T0339137

"You cannot help but read Madden's essays and grin at his deadpan maniacal love for detail and life and kids and anecdotes and wrinkles in the fabric of nominal reality. The guy is obsessed with nominal reality and all the shimmers and windows in it. A terrific essayist, and even better, wholly and utterly unique—there really isn't an essayist today who writes like this, I think, and for all Madden's worshipping of Montaigne, Madden's more interesting and absorbing and funny. Heresy! But it's true."
—the late Brian Doyle, author of *One Long River of Song*

PRAISE FOR PATRICK MADDEN'S *SUBLIME PHYSICK*

"No one writing essays today does so with a greater awareness of the genre's literary traditions than Patrick Madden. Irresistible with their meditative musicality and erudite reflections, these essays brilliantly balance a tough-minded pragmatism with a warm embrace of the impossible. Like all the great essayists he pays homage to, Madden seeks to find the miraculous in the mundane, the sublime in the ordinary, the hazards lurking in our momentary contentment. He understands perfectly why Emerson thought the joy of essaying lay in surprise: to surprise their readers, essayists must first surprise themselves."
—Robert Atwan, series editor, Best American Essays

"Reading Madden's meta-writings on his own writing is like listening to a magician revealing his tricks, yet he always holds the upper hand."
—E. V. De Cleyre, *Brevity*

"The essays in *Sublime Physick* are more than self-reflective; they connect internal states with the marvelous world."
—Renée E. D'Aoust, *Inside Higher Ed*

"A collection of moments that culminate in lives both exalted and ordinary."
—Amanda Forbes Silva, *Ploughshares*

"To read a Patrick Madden essay is to interface with the mind of an engaged, self-conscious thinker. Actually, that's not quite right: it is to interface with Madden's curation of the minds of many thinkers within the expanse of his own."
—John Proctor, *Numéro Cinq*

"Capricious yet erudite . . . In making new connections, Madden creates an obscure kind of beauty."
—Alexandra Masters, *Times Literary Supplement*

"Patrick Madden combines, to a rare degree, a scholar's knowledge and an artist's command of the essay as a literary form. In his hands, the essay becomes a medium for pondering and celebrating our mysterious existence. Readers who wish to reflect more deeply on their own lives will find abundant rewards in these pages."
—Scott Russell Sanders, author of *Earth Works: Selected Essays*

"Ingenious and witty, audacious and charming, learned, moving, and frank: Patrick Madden's *Sublime Physick* places him among the most interesting and essential essayists of our time."
—Mary Cappello, author of *Awkward: A Detour* and *Called Back*

"It's like Montaigne and Sebald got drunk and wrote a book together."
—Brian Doyle, author of *Mink River* and *Leaping*

PRAISE FOR PATRICK MADDEN'S *QUOTIDIANA*

"Patrick Madden has a footloose, restless, well-stocked mind, sometimes maddening but always quite interesting; he gleefully demonstrates what Montaigne claimed: an essay is the best way to show that everything is connected to everything else."
—Phillip Lopate, editor of *The Art of the Personal Essay*

"Words form constellations; they glitter on the pages. . . . There is a religiosity here, though not the usual kind. It's a glow on the horizon, a low light, something to think our way toward."
—Susan Salter Reynolds, *Los Angeles Times*

"At once an approachable and postmodern composition, *Quotidiana* presents an enthralled, reflexive mind at work. Readers will eagerly await [Madden's] next thought."
—Janelle Adsit, *Foreword Reviews*

DISPARATES

DISPA

RATES

Essays

PATRICK MADDEN

University of Nebraska Press   Lincoln

Acknowledgments for the use of
copyrighted material appear on
pages xvii–xviii, which constitute an
extension of the copyright page.

Publication of this volume was
assisted by a grant from the Friends
of the University of Nebraska Press.

Library of Congress
Cataloging-in-Publication Data
Names: Madden, Patrick, 1971– author.
Title: Disparates: essays /
Patrick Madden.
Description: Lincoln: University
of Nebraska Press, [2020].
Identifiers: LCCN 2019039055
ISBN 9781496202444 (paperback)
ISBN 9781496221865 (epub)
ISBN 9781496221872 (mobi)
ISBN 9781496221889 (pdf)
Subjects: LCSH: American essays.
Classification: LCC PS3613.A28355
A6 2020 | DDC 814/.6—dc23
LC record available at https://
lccn.loc.gov/2019039055

Designed and set in
Arno by N. Putens.

For my parents, Pat and Liz (1946–2016), with love

The ideas of humankind and the human soul are pure disparates. Really, all our beliefs, our knowledge, and our arrogance are disparates. Thus the disparate is the sincerest form of literature.

—RAMÓN GOMEZ DE LA SERNA, "Theory of the Disparate"

The form, too, admits variety. The essay can be short or long, serious or trifling, about God and Spinoza, or about turtles and Cheapside . . . The principle which controls it is simply that it should give pleasure.

—VIRGINIA WOOLF, "The Modern Essay"

[The essay] starts not with Adam and Eve but with what it wants to talk about; it says what occurs to it in that context and stops when it feels finished . . . Hence it is classified as a trivial endeavor.

—THEODOR ADORNO, "The Essay as Form"

CONTENTS (MAY HAVE SHIFTED)

ABORTED ESSAYS

> What abortions are these Essays! What errors, what
> ill-pieced transitions, what crooked reasons, what lame
> conclusions! How little is made out, and that little how ill!
> —WILLIAM HAZLITT, "The Indian Jugglers"

LYRIC ESSAYS

Every time I hear *lyric essay*, I think of Rodgers and Hart. The Great American Essay Book. My funny Emerson. Sweet comic Emerson. You make me smile with your pompous transcendental insights.

—DAVID LAZAR, "Hydra: I'll Be Your Mirror"

GUERRILLA ESSAYS

As those who by artificial light put out that of the day, so we, by borrowed forms, have destroyed our own.

—MONTAIGNE, "Of the Custom of Wearing Clothes"

CONTENTS (IN ORDER OF APPEARANCE)

ILLUSTRATIONS

ACKNOWLEDGMENTS

> The true proficiency of the soul consists not so much in deep thinking
> or eloquent speaking or beautiful writing as in much and warm loving.
> —SANTA TERESA DE AVILA, "On the Love of God"

Writing a book is an exhilarating task, mostly because of the connections I'm able to make, among experiences and ideas and people, which all feel like forms of love. So, although there is a single name on the cover, I cannot credit myself solely or indeed very much for the results.

A glance at the table of contents reveals that we have made explicit something that is always implicit in books (especially essay collections): the vital assistance of others. Here I have relied on the featured contributions of Lawrence Sutin, Lina María Ferreira Cabeza-Vanegas, Jericho Parms, Amy Leach, Desirae Matherly, Joe Oestreich, David Lazar, Elena Passarello, Wendy S. Walters, Stephen Haynie, Michael Martone, Joni Tevis, Matthew Gavin Frank, and Mary Cappello. I love how they've transformed my essays in unexpected and playful ways, and I thank them for their creative generosity.

But this is not my first foray into such collaboration. In my previous book, *Sublime Physick*, I wrote a long essay on originality called "Independent Redundancy." I thought it would be clever, as I explored and troubled the concept, positing that all creation is arrangement, all originality is influenced, to invite friends to write passages of the essay mimicking my voice. Instead of me borrowing the preexisting sentences of others, others would create new sentences in my style and offer them freely. Seventeen people agreed to help, with no direct credit and no payment other than a copy of the book. Since (to my knowledge) nobody has yet discovered this Easter egg, I want to reveal here, with my gratitude, that Sari Carter, Eric Freeze, Brian Doyle, Ned Stuckey-French, Dinty W. Moore, Eric LeMay, Michael

Steinberg, Brian Hoover, John Proctor, Jacob Paul, Elizabeth Rhondeau, Lina María Ferreira Cabeza-Vanegas, William Bradley, Judith Kitchen, Ryan McIlvain, Scott Russell Morris, and Amy Lee Scott are responsible for approximately one-fifth of that essay. See if you can discover their parts (or ask us). I especially acknowledge the following five co-conspirators, whom cancer has taken recently: Judith Kitchen (whose paragraph on p. 211 begins "Of course, when it comes to independent redundancy, writing is unlike music . . ."), William Bradley (who begins on p. 209 with "I recently found myself following the public feud between the producers . . ."), Michael Steinberg (who wrote the section beginning on p. 193 with "which is a topic I've been thinking about a lot lately . . ."), Ned Stuckey-French (p. 184, "And the essay is the literary genre most explicitly focused on subjectivity . . ."), and Brian Doyle (who, it seems to me, couldn't quite disguise himself even when trying to write like me, p. 159: "But to return, sidelong, diligently, like a small child who was going to check out that cool bird's nest in the backyard but got distracted by how hard it is to hop on one foot for more than, say, eight hops . . .").

So many people have contributed to this book in ways both obvious and oblivious; it would be impossible to thank them all. Nevertheless, I thank Scott Russell Morris for his beautiful photographs and Brent Rowland for his photo and video work. My wonderful children and wife drew the whimsical pictures to accompany my proverbs. Songwriters Glen Phillips, Ben Huggins, Sebastian Teysera, Felix Luna, and Bob Seger have all given me inspiration (as have many others). Foremost among them is Neil Peart, who died just before this book's publication, and whose lyrics have shaped my thinking and enjoyment of life in myriad ways. I rely constantly on my friends, students, and teachers, and I thank them all, most especially David Lazar and John Bennion, who taught me how to essay.

Of course, the people who inspire me most and who keep teaching me how to essay, daily, are the members of my family. I have dedicated this book to my parents, Pat and Liz, my father still living and my mother gone from this earth in 2016. I miss her profoundly, and I am edified by the essayistic conversations he and I often have.

I thank my siblings and their families: Kathleen, Soren; David, Liz, Brooks; Dan, Ivy, Maverick, Monroe; and my in-laws: Uber, Teresa; Fernando, Ivan, Thiago, Joaquin; Graciela, David, Tiziana, Augusto, Milos; and Valeria and Alejandro for their love and support. Most of all, I am eternally indebted to and eternally grateful for my wife, Karina, the love of my life, and our six no-longer-so-little ones: Pato, Adi, Sara, Dani, Marcos, and James. They are my everything, my sine qua non, that from which all proceeds.

The University of Nebraska Press has always treated me and my books with respect and grace, and I am deeply grateful for their attention and enthusiasm for literature. I especially thank Alicia Christensen, who shepherded this book, and her predecessors, Kristen Elias Rowley and Ladette Randolph, who did the same for my previous books.

I have been blessed beyond my merits by Brigham Young University, which, in addition to providing me employment in a supportive and inspiring atmosphere, allowed me a sabbatical to focus on writing this book. I value my associations with friends, colleagues, and students there and at Vermont College of Fine Arts. I am grateful for the generosity of the George A. and Eliza Gardner Howard Foundation, which granted me a fellowship that also helped me complete this book. I thank everyone who reviewed, recognized, excerpted, awarded, or invited me to read from my previous books, especially the Independent Publisher Book Awards, *Foreword Reviews* Indies Awards, the Council of Literary Magazines and Presses, the Association for Mormon Letters, Artists of Utah, PEN Center USA, and the Association for Writers and Writing Programs.

Many of the essays herein have been published previously in journals, and I thank their editors for their show of faith in my work.

"Writer Michael Martone's Leftover Water: Imbibe literary genius (dozens of authors) in one swig!" *The Normal School* 3.2 (Fall 2010): 37–42.
"Nostalgia." *The Tusculum Review* 10 (2014): 59–61.
"Insomnia" as "Of Eagles, Goats, and Space Men." *The Normal School* 1.1 (Fall 2008): 5.

"Unpredictable Essays." *The Normal School* 11.2 (Fall 2018): 96–98.

"Laughter" as "Off Chairs." *Ocean State Review* 5.1 (Spring 2015): 22–25.

"Happiness." *The Austin Review* 1 (Winter 2014): 125–27.

"Memory" & "Poetry." *Superstition Review* 8 (Fall 2011).

"Mea Culpa." *Brevity* blog. 17 May 2010.

"Expectations." *Superstition Review* blog. 20 April 2017.

"In Step with . . . Montaigne" with David Lazar. *Essay Daily*. 21 October 2015.

"Timing" as "Patrick Madden visite la tour de Montaigne." *Brevity* blog. 15 April 2014.

"Inertia." *Miracle Monocle* 9 (Spring 2017).

"Thumbs." *Fourth Genre* 11.1 (Spring 2009): 125–39.

"Distance." *Passages North*. 22 October 2013.

"Against the Wind" as "The Bidet Towel." *Sphere* 44 (2000): 64–65.

"Aborted Essay on Plums." *Sweet: A Literary Confection* 9.2 (January 2017).

"Solstice" as "What Happened on April 21, 2018." *Essay Daily*. 8 July 2018.

"Listening." *Essay Daily*. 14 December 2016.

A book seems like a finite, completed thing, but of course it lives and expands in readers' minds, where it is always a different version of itself, so that very quickly the idea of unity becomes . . . questionable. To further that question and to further interact with readers, I've created some online bonus materials, including additional Dickens and Brontë comma-then examples (see "The Arrogance of Style"), a randomly generated "Laughter" essay in need of your humorous anecdotes, advice about creating your own WordSearch essays (see "Repast"), and everything you need to write additional Botnik-powered predictive-text essays seeded with my books or other source texts (see "Unpredictable Essays"). Visit http://quotidiana.org/disparates/ to join in the fun. And thank you for reading.

disparate /ˈdɪspərət/ [Latin *disparātus* (separated, divided), past participle of *disparāre*, from *dis-*(apart) + *parāre* (to prepare, provide, contrive); also associated with Latin *dispar* (unequal, unlike, different).]

†**2.** noun, chiefly plural. Diverse, unequal, incongruous things, words, ideas.

2020 MADDEN *Disp*. xix An essay collection is by definition made of disparates, miscellaneous ingredients held together loosely by voice or style or abstract ideas. **2020** MADDEN *Disp*. xix Despite efforts by publishers to thematize and memoirize nonfiction books for promotional purposes, disparate essay collections stubbornly refuse to vanish (thank goodness). **2020** MADDEN *Disp*. xix Such that what follows herein is unavoidably disparate, whether by design or failure or authorial inability to meet the market's demands. **2020** MADDEN *Disp*. xix But this is not the sense in which I most wish to explore the concept of disparates.

disparate /dɪspɑˈrɑteɪ/ [Spanish *disparate* (nonsense, foolishness), from *disparatar* (intr. to say or do something beyond reason); also associated with *disparar* (tr. to shoot or throw violently; to leave precipitously).]

1. noun. Absurdity, inanity, frivolity; nonsense, claptrap, rubbish; balderdash, malarkey, drivel.

2020 MADDEN *Disp*. xix Having lived in Uruguay for many years, and being married to a Uruguayan for over two decades, I have become accustomed to hearing (and have often been accused of saying) disparates. **2020** MADDEN *Disp*. xix Understanding full well that the term is usually not an approbation but a pejorative, I nevertheless borrow the affirmative, ironic sense of *disparate*, where such statements are good, often humorous, even healthy, certainly anti-polemical. **2020** MADDEN *Disp.* xx What's more, given my penchant for titling books after essays' quiddities (their quotidianness, their sublimation of the physical), I find that *disparates* serves the pattern well. **1994** GALEANO *Amér. libre.* VII 12 I believe that this book [*Walking Words*] is a disparate that comes from the collective imagination. **2020** MADDEN *Disp.* xx For have not essays always been concerned with disparates: (seeming) trivialities, absurdities, inanities, flippancies? **2020** MADDEN *Disp.* xx And are not essays *themselves* often accused of being only disparates, inconclusive attempts at humble exploration without any materialistic ends? **2020** MADDEN *Disp.* xx Yet do we not know that essays are truly of utmost importance, providing respite from or a meandering pathway through the disparate [here I use the word straight, without irony] that is this toiling, moiling world? **1881** STEVENSON *Virg. Puer.* 126 Extreme *busyness* . . . is a symptom of deficient vitality; and a faculty for idleness implies a catholic appetite and a strong sense of [the disparate]. **2020** MADDEN *Disp.* xx Indeed, from the essay's beginnings, a book such as this was conceived as a disparate in both the English and Spanish senses: a miscellany to be sampled and savored, without order or organization, without rhyme or reason. **1580** MONTAIGNE *Essays* I *xxviii* 164 What are these things of mine, in truth, but grotesques and monstrous [disparates], pieced together of divers members, without definite shape, having no order, sequence, or proportion other than accidental? **2020** MADDEN *Disp.* xx Thus in these pages I attempt to reassert the value of the disparate, which controverts reason, which shakes our certainties, which lightens our burdens, which alleviates our sorrows and brings us to laughter (of insight or humor) as it sidesteps "reality" to create a reality in which art and idle thought are worthy pursuits, worthier, indeed, than all our getting. **2020** MADDEN *Disp.* xx Such are the twenty-two etchings in Francisco de Goya's *Disparates* series, depicting phantasmagorical scenes of half-real, half-imaginary follies ("Fearful folly," "Flying folly," "Furious folly," "Merry folly," etc.), including my favorite, which I see as a metaphor for this collection: "*Disparate ridículo*," in which a group of figures huddles

on a tree branch, perhaps listening to a philosophizing essayist (with his hand gesturing a point). **2020** MADDEN *Disp.* xxi This particular *Disparate* calls to my mind the criticism that one (an essayist, for sure) is "going off into the branches" instead of sticking close to the trunk, or the core argument; also, of course, it is foolish for the crowd to weigh down the slendering end of the branch, which is sure to break under their weight; I find in the image a joyful metaphor for essaying. **2020** MADDEN *Disp.* xxi Thus even, or especially, without a pragmatic purpose or cogent argument, without a direct engagement of social ills or attempt to right wrongs, the essays herein may (I hope) provide a profound value to readers, or at least to those who know not to disparage the disparate. **2020** MADDEN *Disp.* xxi And just as the term *disparate* is often used as a dismissal, which becomes an invitation to the right hearer or reader, I shall end with Montaigne's disparate: "Thus, reader, I am myself the matter of my book; you would be unreasonable to spend your leisure on so frivolous and vain a subject."

DISPARATES

Writer Michael Martone's Leftover Water

Imbibe literary genius (dozens of authors) in one swig!

You are bidding on approximately 8.3 ounces of Dasani water (plus backwash) in a 20-ounce plastic Dasani bottle (lot number NOV0909 TOC0931L3). This was left by writer Michael Martone on Wednesday, March 25, 2009, after a reading at Brigham Young University, during which Martone read the "Contributor's Note" where he talks about his mother writing his school assignments, "G♯ Minor 7th in the Second Inversion," and "Seventeen Postcards from Terra Incognita."

Why should you want Michael Martone's leftover water, especially when Elvis's may come up for bid again? You may recall from one of Martone's "Contributor's Notes" that

> in his role as host of a reading, he is often faced with what to do with the leftover water of his guests. . . . Martone is left behind to secure the room, coil the microphone cables, clean up, kill the lights. Part of the cleaning up part has always included the disposing of the evening's water. Often the lecture halls and auditoriums are not outfitted with a sink. Indeed, the whole point of the headache of providing water in the first place has been the fact that the hall is not in close proximity to sources of water. So Martone has found that he has fallen into the habit of finishing the water himself, drinking the dregs from the glasses or bottles left by the readers like a priest ingesting the leftover Eucharist at the end of Mass. Martone does this more out of a sense of neatness and order, but, he supposes, there is some

of the spirit involved as well. He has witnessed some really amazing performances, listened to the work of famous and remarkably gifted writers. And he has drunk their leftover water. Perhaps a part of him believes some of that talent and skill will find its way into his own metabolism through this communion with greatness. It is a kind of inoculation, by means of this tainted fluid, with the cooties of the greatest. Martone hopes, as he drinks, that its inspirational properties, if not the medicinal ones, have "taken."

So, you're securing decades' worth of literary genius—"the cooties of the greatest"—all at once, through the cooties of this pioneering collector. Whose DNA might you find swirling in this literary stew? Gordon Lish, Tobias Wolff, Mary Karr, David Foster Wallace, William Gass, Jane Smiley, Lewis Hyde, Susan Dodd, Susan Neville, Tony Early, Louise Glück, Dean Young, Louise Erdrich, Charles Baxter, AND MORE! Plus, with over eight ounces of the muse-juice, you can pass it around at your next writers' group meeting and still have liquid to spare. Save it a few years, collect other writers' backwash, spit in it yourself, resell it on eBay and make your money back, do what you want to do: you bought it; it's yours.

Whatever you do with it—whether you gulp it down in one swig, savor it a sip at a time, share it with friends, or simply place it as a trophy on your writing desk—you may be assured of immediate inspiration and better literary output, followed by fame and adulation, and most likely a hefty advance on your next book, not to mention the royalties from the movie version, starring Sean Penn and Winona Ryder.*

In addition to this priceless H_2O, the winning bidder will also receive a handwritten Postcard of Authenticity from Michael Martone congratulating him/her on his/her wise investment and certifying that the leftover water is indeed Martone's.

*Results may vary; seller makes no guarantee, expressed or implied, of literary potion's actual effectiveness at making your writing better.

Q: Does Martone floss?

A: Allow me, instead, to answer the questions I think you're really asking: 1) Did Martone floss soon before drinking, thereby limiting the quantity of valuable food morsels floating in the water? A: No, he did not. The water is sufficiently infested. 2) Why is flossing important? A: If you're like me, then you may floss occasionally, when you remember and aren't too tired, without much gusto. But hear ye my sad tale: Now I've got "deep pockets"—and not the kind that begets prodigal spending—which means "deep cleaning" from the dentist, which hurts and requires quarterly instead of biannual visits, which most insurance companies won't quite cover, which does some damage to those "shallow pockets" most writers have, which brings up this interesting note from the dictionary—"floss: v. intr. to flirt; to show off, esp. (in later use) by flaunting one's wealth, possessions, etc."—a thing Michael Martone most certainly does not do.

Q: I'd like to inquire about the safety of this product . . . has Martone been tested for insanity and other transmittable mental conditions?

A: You are hoping, perhaps, to catch some of what he has? Some of that "benign neurosis" (to borrow a phrase from George Higgins) called "writing"? That's understandable. It is, after all, a rare individual who will hole up for hours, conversing only with himself, spinning stories and ideas from gossamer words, lining them up neatly (or putting them in a cage to fight to the death), straining for communication. If at the microscopic level our atoms never quite touch, then maybe words and diseases are all we have to reach one another.

Q: Are there any visible signs of Martone's interaction with the water bottle (floating particles, teethmarks on the cap from opening it, etc.)?

A: I submit into evidence the video stills of Martone drinking from this very bottle of water. From that point to now, I will submit my own spotless record of honesty and truth-telling, even down to my choice of literary genre. Dr. Martone has also agreed to send to the winner a handwritten Postcard of Authenticity suitable

for framing or recycling. Of course, you are free to hire your own forensics expert to verify the water bottle's authenticity. Next time you see Martone, simply pluck one of his long gray hairs to get your DNA match. As for the other writers whose germs are also likely swimming in this swill, you'll simply have to believe Martone. We do.

Q: Would it be possible for Martone to personalize the Postcard of Authenticity?
A: Ooh yeah. It's a handwritten postcard from Michael Martone telling you A) that the water is authentic; B) that you're awesome; C) don't drink it all now—save some for later.

Q: How will you ship this leftover water of Michael Martone? Will certain precautions be taken, it being not just water, which is, speaking from personal experience, tricky enough to ship, but also a unique collector's item? Thank you for your time.
A: In order to keep would-be mail thieves off the trail of this valuable and unique collector's item/literary potency potion, I will

mail the bottle, padded by Styrofoam "peanuts" or bubble wrap, in an inconspicuous corrugated cardboard box of indeterminate dimensions. Contrarily, I am happy to simply spill the water in a major river upstream from you, at a preappointed time, or to simply leave the bottle uncapped outside in the sun for several days so the water evaporates and rejoins the Great Cycle of Life, to then rain down and bless the earth and her inhabitants with deeply moving ideas and inspirations (I'll have to charge a little extra to do my rain dance to make the winds blow the clouds from Utah toward your home).

Q: What color is the water?

A: Color, when understood beyond the sixty-four-variety Crayola box, is essentially the eye/brain's perception of a certain wavelength range of electromagnetic radiation (approximately 390 nm–730 nm), which we call visible light. An object's color, then, basically consists of the wavelengths of light that it reflects or transmits (as opposed to absorbs). Other factors, such as viewing angle, reflectiveness, or source-light, can also influence color perception. In the case of water, small amounts, such as the approximately 8.3 ounces offered here for auction, tend to be viewed as "clear." Yet, as you no doubt remember from your high school physics course, water tends to absorb the longer wavelengths of light (the red end of the visible spectrum) while allowing the shorter wavelengths (blues) to pass through. This effect is enhanced by particulates suspended or dissolved in the water. Water may also reflect ambient light (from the sky, the table it's placed upon), thus offering the curious viewer a soothing spectrum of grays or browns. I highly recommend viewing your Michael Martone water in a variety of settings and under a variety of circumstances. Perhaps the most rewarding would be this: place a shining flashlight horizontally in a darkened room. Face the same direction as your flashlight beam, a few steps to the side. Hold your Michael Martone water at arm's length in front of you at a forty-five-degree angle. Turn the bottle, tilt it a little this way, a little that way, raise it, lower it, to find the optimal viewing position. Soon you should see, on the right side of the water, a red sliver; soon you will recognize the rainbow! And thus we see that Michael Martone's leftover water is all colors.

Q: I have seen the pictures of Michael Martone you have posted. How can I be sure that the Michael Martone who gave the reading was the Michael Martone who wrote the book *Michael Martone*? Does the Michael Martone who will write the Postcard of Authenticity of the water come with any kind of certificate that he is indeed Michael Martone or *the* Michael Martone?

A: "But how do I know that there is not something different altogether from the objects I have now enumerated, of which it is impossible to entertain the slightest doubt? Is there not a God, or some being, by whatever name I may designate him, who causes these thoughts to arise in my mind? But why suppose such a being, for it may be I myself am capable of producing them? Am I, then, at least not something? But I before denied that I possessed senses or a body; I hesitate, however, for what follows from that? Am I so dependent on the body and the senses that without these I cannot exist? But I had the persuasion that there was absolutely nothing in the world, that there was no sky and no earth, neither minds nor bodies; was I not, therefore, at the same time, persuaded that I did not exist? Far from it; I assuredly existed, since I was persuaded. But there is I know not what being, who is possessed at once of the highest power and the deepest cunning, who is constantly employing all his ingenuity in deceiving me. Doubtless, then, I exist, since I am deceived; and, let him deceive me as he may, he can never bring it about that I am nothing, so long as I shall be conscious that I am something. So that it must, in fine, be maintained, all things being maturely and carefully considered, that this proposition (pronunciatum) I am, I exist, is necessarily true each time it is expressed by me, or conceived in my mind."

Q: Is this your only Martone item or will you be auctioning other collectibles? I'm most interested in Martone's water from AWP conferences, or pieces of toast with the burnt silhouette of his pompadour . . .

A: Thank you for bidding and asking this intriguing question, though I have to take issue with your characterization of Martone's hairstyle. The pompadour, which I've just researched a tad, is short on the sides, combed up in front and back on top, forming a kind of smoothly rounded forehead shelf. Think Elvis, Roy Orbison, James Dean. If you're interested in making your own pompadour (while you still can; I'm beyond this possibility), you may find helpful instructions online, including videos on YouTube. Additionally, you may find it interesting/frustrating to learn that the pompadour is named for Jeanne-Antoinette Poisson, Marquise de Pompadour, who was King Louis XV's mistress in the mid-eighteenth century. Did she wear her hair like this? Not according to the portraits. So why do we trace the etymology of the hairstyle to her? Because "she introduced these styles." Whuh? To make a long story short: I am hoping the exclusivity of this Martone Memorabilia will send its auction price skyrocketing. I have nothing else to auction (at this time).

Q: This is delicate, but I have to ask. Does Martone ever sell other fluids, as in . . . fluids, you know, that have already passed through certain of his bodily channels? I don't want to come right out and name what I'm looking for, but you get my drift?

A: You mean tears? You must mean tears. I can't think of anything else you might be referring to. The good news is, YES, I believe I recall Martone, moved by his own poetical prose, eyes glistening, a drop meandering slowly from his moist ducts to the tip of his nose, gathering mass, tensing, testing the limits of molecular cohesion until, in the exact moment that he unscrewed the cap of his twenty-ounce Dasani water bottle, the teardop dripped and dropped—plop—right into the open mouth of the vessel.

Q: In a previous question you refer to him as "Dr. Martone." When I graduated from his program, last year, he was Michael Martone,

MA. What institution within the past year granted the great one his doctorate? And what is he now a doctor in? Is he a real doctor (the medical kind)?

A: You're very observant! The truth is, there are plenty of "doctors" who don't have doctorates or medical licenses. To wit: Dr. Pat Robertson, Dr. Johnson, Dr. Demento. Samuel Johnson, for instance, left Oxford without a degree and though his friends long sought to obtain for him some document of his erudition, he received his master's only just before he published his monumental Dictionary of the English Language in 1755 (he was forty-six). His honorary doctorate degrees came a decade and two later, long after he'd acquired his honorific nickname. William Hazlitt didn't much like Dr. Johnson's writings, but James Boswell sure did: "Had Dr. Johnson written his own life, in conformity with the opinion which he has given, that every man's life may be best written by himself; had he employed in the preservation of his own history, that clearness of narration and elegance of language in which he has embalmed so many eminent persons, the world would probably have had the most perfect example of biography that was ever exhibited. But although he at different times, in a desultory manner, committed to writing many particulars of the progress of his mind and fortunes, he never had persevering diligence enough to form them into a regular composition." This is just fine by us. He wrote essays, not memoir. Super. Anyway, who'll be the first university to confer an honorary doctorate on Michael Martone? Perhaps it'll be Brigham Young. I'll ask.

Q: I'm interested in acquiring the Martone water for my rare waters collection. But I'd like to know, where did the water originally come from? I'd appreciate any information you can share about its origins.

A: Leaving aside impossible questions of "origins" for the moment, the water in Martone's water bottle was taken from the Atlanta, Georgia, public water supply before it was purified by "reverse osmosis" (essentially straining through a filter) and "enhanced" with trace amounts of magnesium sulfate, potassium chloride, and salt (sodium chloride). The Coca-Cola company, which brings us Dasani water, assures us that "DASANI is water—pure and essential. DASANI helps you embrace life with a fresh, optimistic outlook. As basic as breathing, DASANI quenches thirst naturally and deliciously." I'm feeling better already. [Do they realize that they're claiming that Dasani is as basic as breathing?] As for the origins of water on the earth, well, even Wikipedia doesn't quite know the answer, so I can't help you there. I will say, though, that thank goodness there *is* water on the earth, or how could we live!

Q: What is it with universities in the western United States that they must put an initial on the side of a mountain face overlooking the campus below?

A: Sheer boredom.

Q: I collect Dasani products and Dasani-brand memorabilia. Michael Martone I'm not familiar with. Can you please provide more details about the bottle itself? Thank you!

A: I'm glad to know that this item has broad appeal to all sorts of collectors. The bottle at one time contained 20 fluid ounces OR 1.25 pints OR 591 milliliters of water. Now, not quite so much, because this Martone fellow drank a bit more than half. The bottle is roughly a cylinder, tapered at the top into a narrow spout, with five "knobs" at the bottom, for greater stability. The bottle measures approximately 8 inches high and 3⅝ inches at its largest diameter. It is made of relatively clear Polyethylene Terephthalate, with a translucent blue shrink band around its middle. This band says such things as "Dasani," "a product of the Coca-Cola Company" (in script), "NON-CARBONATED crisp, fresh taste. Dasani is filtered through a state-of-the-art purification system and enhanced with minerals for a pure, clean taste that can't be beat" (I'll say; not when you mix in the remnants of the best literary minds of our nascent century!).

You can get a cash refund for this bottle in California; you can get five cents for it in Hawaii and Maine; but you cannot get a refill. The plastic above the blue band is decorated with relief patterns in the Art Deco style. Between two parallel bands of two outdentations each, we find the cypher "sososososo-soso," which one might easily take to be a cry for help until one notices that there is no second s; therefore one is forced to conclude that the sculpture is a comment on the content, that it is "so so." Above this declaration of mediocrity, we find four large S figures marching counter-clockwise as a symbol of the Coca-Cola company's disregard of what is trendy or faddish, like selling bottled water. Finally, atop it all, there is a blue cap, separated from its still-present blue safety band. The cap includes around its circumference twenty-four grooves to help you open the bottle, plus a few more decorative esses up top. It is a fine, fine specimen indeed.

Q: You suggested that Martone's water might do well as a trophy to be displayed on a something such as a desk. But don't you think that it might feel more at home in a well-lit, specially designed cabinet complete with a plush velvet cushion lined in gold trim? If interested, please send me a query denoting any other decorative flourishes you have in mind. As for the cabinet's security, I have some big ideas that involve a special heat-&-nose–hair-activated locking system. (Note: the laser-printed display plaque would come free of charge!)

A: This is the thing about which I am talking! If we, as a race of bipedal, opposable-thumbed, wondering, pondering creatures, have thus far limited ourselves to Velcro shoe fasteners and decorative lunchboxes, then we have surely missed our poten-tial. Just imagine what wonders we might yet discover/invent if we combine our ideas and our skills to fashion a world in which seemingly ordinary, even disposable things are given their proper due as miracles of existence without which life would remain empty or perhaps only just under half full, approximately

8.3 ounces out of a possible 20, let's say. But with collaboration and ingenuity, plus maybe a little bit of capital supplied by the great worldwide garage sale that is eBay, we can subvert our species' most widespread and more wrongheaded notions. What was it that Montaigne said? (Don't worry; I'll tell you; just let me look it up.) He said, "From the most ordinary, commonplace, familiar things, if we could put them in their proper light, can be formed the greatest miracles of nature and the most wondrous examples." And what was it that Charles Caleb Colton said? He sent a tribute to you, dear questioner: "Some men of a secluded and studious life have sent forth from their closet or their cloister, rays of intellectual light that have agitated courts and revolutionized kingdoms; like the moon which, though far removed from the ocean, and shining upon it with a serene and sober light, is the chief cause of all those ebbings and flowings which incessantly disturb that restless world of waters." (You will forgive the gendered language of that benighted past, I pray.)

Q: Besides that it belonged to and was sipped upon by Michael Martone (who himself has sipped upon the water of many illustrious writers), is there anything else that makes this particular water unique? Does it have an interesting smell, for example? Is it somehow wetter than normal water? Will it make a strange sound when swished or gargled?

A: The only way I know of to test water for wetness is to bathe in it, so that's what I did (making sure to funnel the resultant drip back into the bottle), and, sure enough, it's wet! Perhaps it's even wetter than the water I usually get from my shower, I don't know. While bathing, I also took the opportunity to sniff the stuff, which seems not to smell like anything but water. By the way, I do not recommend "sniffing" water, as the liquid cannot be processed by human lungs, the oxygen in the water molecule remaining stubbornly attached to its two hydrogens. In my case, my organism reacted rather violently to the introduction of H_2O

into my nasal cavity, causing me to quickly jerk and sneeze the water back out of my nose, along with a collection of sputum that I'd been harboring in the upper reaches. This, too, was collected back into the bottle, which I then swished and gargled, to test your hypothesis about strange sounds. I have good news to report: Whether it was the water or my wife, there were certainly strange gagging sounds accompanying my experiment. What's more, with these tests I seem to have increased the volume of liquid in the bottle nearly 0.2 ounces! Talk about more for your money!

Q: A few years ago at the AWP in Austin, Michael Martone was played by one of his students. The student gave Michael Martone's reading, wore Michael Martone's nametag, and generally put across the idea that *he was* Michael Martone. My question, then, is: how do we know that this water touched the REAL Michael Martone's lips? Certainly your pictures and your postcard could be faked. And then if I were to drink this water, I would not be imbibing literary greatness, which would inspire in me great works of the pen, but con-artist greatness, which might inspire me to great works of the short or long con. Are you okay with this potential life of crime should your product be a fake?

A: The quick answer is Yes! Whether literary genius or criminal/mischievous proclivities, it is all the same to me. I walk away with my $21.50, minus posting and purchase fees to both eBay and PayPal, and laugh my way to the bank. But your question takes me beyond my good friend Descartes, to whom I've already recurred. Did you know: A quick, superficial search for "Michael Martone" on http://switchboard.com/ produces phone numbers and/or addresses for up to eighty-one individuals? Michael Martones populate many of our fifty states, though it would seem, from a cursory glance at the data, that most of them reside in the Northeast. In Alabama, last known residence of the Michael Martone in question, there is only one, which thereby proves my contention that this water was indeed sipped by *the* Michael Martone, *quod erat demonstrandum.* If you're still not convinced, try a Google images search for "Michael Martone" (in quotation marks). Then try it without the quotation marks. Either way, the results are the same: along the top row of recollected images, we find a picture of former vice president of the United States Dan Quayle, known mostly for his boyish good looks and spelling difficulties. There are also, within the first page of results, a picture of a strapping young man on Facebook and/or a Michigan judge. A judge would simply get himself into too much trouble impersonating a well-known writer. And thus we see that whether this water be authentic or not, even the *real* Michael Martone is quite a literary huckster, so you're exposing yourself to a conniver's germs either way. What an adventure!

Q: Clearly, the leftover water of Michael Martone, writer, is worth many times more than its value when purchased from, say, a 7-Eleven. Does the seller have plans for what to do with his money?

A: All profits will be used for the advancement and glorification of the essay in the world.

Q: Do you have any suggestions for distilling the writing-enhancing particulates of Martone et al. from the water so that a successful bidder might turn this little plastic factory into a goldmine through massive synthetic reproduction of said particulates? Also, does "Writer Michael Martone's Leftover Water" have any effect on pets?

A: Your second question first: The seller makes no warranty, expressed or implied, about Writer Michael Martone's Leftover Water's effect on pets. That said, sure! Give it a try! There's those painting elephants and sign-language-using gorillas, so why not!? As for successfully distilling writerly particulates: I recommend you boil the liquid at exactly one hundred degrees Celsius until all the water has vaporized. In your pot, you should find a whitish film. Carefully scrape this caked-on residue with your index fingernail, then soak your contaminated finger in a new bottle of water for seven minutes or until the white film has dissolved completely. Repeat this process until your pot is completely clean. I suspect you can make several gallons of WriterWater at a concentration of nineteen to twenty-three parts per million. Good luck!

Q: As you insinuated before, by drinking this water we may imbibe greatness. I had questions about that greatness. Does the greatness get better with age? If it does increase in genius quality is it like a fine wine or is it like an old parchment? If I win the bid, would you suggest drinking the water right away so as to acquire the amalgamated greatness or should I let the water age and drink it after a year or two?

A: The great thing about literary greatness is that it *does* improve with age. What's even greater is that this greatness greatens whether it's sitting in a bottle in your trophy case or coursing through your veins. Except in cases of dementia or self-plagiarism, literary greatness continues to grow until death (in some cases, even after death). So go ahead and drink up now. (By the way, I notice that you haven't actually bid on the water; you won't be drinking anything if you don't pony up!)

Q: Been talking to a buddy of mine about the possibility of cloning Dr. Martone using the DNA left behind in the dry spit on the top of that bottle of water you got. Think that will work? Also, perhaps we can clone the DNA of the other writers who swim in Dr. Martone's spit. Don't you imagine?

A: Imagine all the people!

Q: In the head-on picture of (not yet Dr.) Martone drinking from the item, his expression is clearly one of barely suppressed rage. I was wondering if you have any knowledge about what so ignited his fury. I've often heard him described as a rather gentle, genial being, but evidently that's not the whole story. Do you have the whole story?

A: As you have suggested, there is always more to the story. To understand Martone's apparent "fury," we would do well to consult the Oracle (Internet) to trace the etymology of that term. It turns out that the Furies were born from the severed genitalia of Uranus, long, long ago. According to the Iliad, their purpose is to "punish whoever has sworn a false oath," which once again confirms this auction's fundamental claim that the water is legitimately Michael Martone's. Beyond  that, and leaving aside for a moment all talk of vengeance and snake-hair, Wikipedia assures us that "[The Furies] represent regeneration and the potency of creation, which both consumes and empowers." This is an apt description of literary genius, no? I would like to add that R.E.M. lyrics are often very difficult to decipher, but I once did a pretty decent job of figuring out "It's the End of the World as We Know It (and I Feel Fine)," which includes the line about "the Furies breathing down your neck." This may have been my first encounter with the Furies, though perhaps not with fury. I have a friend whose brother, instead of giving an actual valedictory "speech" to his graduating high school class, stood at the podium and sang this very song from start to finish, then just sat down. I don't think I would have had the guts to do that. In fact, I didn't. I made a reference to the students in Tiananmen Square, basically saying that we, the Whippany Park High School class of 1989, had it easy, so we should try to *do* something with our lives. And here I am, doing this auction.

Nostalgia (feat. Lawrence Sutin)

Were I to write a Baconian or Emersonian essay on nostalgia, I'd hope to arrive at something gnomic, like Joaquin Sabina:

No hay nostalgia peor que añorar lo que nunca jamás sucedió

which is to say, "There is no worse nostalgia than longing for what never happened," which I don't entirely understand, though it has the ring of truth to it, or perhaps its phrasing disarms rational counterargument, which is something like the definition of *gnomic*, from the Greek *gnōmikos*: "thought, judgment," but with a twist toward the enigmatic and ambiguous. "The ring of truth" is a phrase I first heard in my high school physics class with Mr. Altenderfer. It was the name of a PBS science miniseries hosted by Philip Morrison, a gnomic fellow, as I remember him, though I thought it then a comment on his stature more than on his mysteriousness. Had he a long beard and toque the image would be complete, but he wore no such things in the show, so, I realize now, my comment is entirely linguistic, a formation of the essay itself, a happily accidental result of my choice to invoke the word *gnomic* above. Still, let it stand. He *was* short and, I think now, in love with the earth and gleeful at the limits of knowledge, so the adjective describes him amply, which is what good adjectives do.

I never saw the PBS series but have now and then heard the ring of truth and its fading away. As a lifelong sufferer from nostalgia for what never happened, I will take a crack at explaining this slippery irony. Memory is shaped by desire. Desires often do not take shape. So memories can be, and may often be, fantasies that have taken such strong and recurrent root in our minds that they become memories as we recall them.

Of course, I've just spent entirely too much time watching old *Ring of Truth* clips on YouTube, realizing that I haven't thought of that program for decades, and I retain almost none of it in my conscious memory, but I like to think that it shaped me in small, important ways. It holds up quite well, I think, and I shall likely share it with my children, to inspire in them a sense of wonder at the natural world, a sense that I achieve less often nowadays than when I was young and (as it seems now) carefree. O how I miss that time in Mr. Altenderfer's class, when life was structured and I felt that all I had to do was fit the expectations others set for me, an activity I excelled at. (See how I did that? I hadn't intended to. Initially I thought I would write a whole essay about nostalgia without once waxing nostalgic. I'd remain cool and distanced, maybe utterly metanostalgic.)

The word *gnome* used to describe "diminutive spirits fabled to inhabit the interior of the earth and to be the guardians of its treasures," according to the OED, was coined by Paracelsus, perhaps to mean "earth-dweller" in mistaken Greeky parallel to "sea-dweller," but more likely, free from etymological precursors, just because he could. It is probably not related to the other *gnome*, the pithy maxim one, though I feel it should be.

Just as I feel that everyone should know that the name Paracelsus's parents gave him when he was born in Switzerland the year after Columbus discovered America was Philippus Aureolus Theophrastus Bombastus von Hohenheim, a name beautiful in so many ways and for so many reasons. I can't even begin to parse those tongue-trippingly risible words! My haltingly peripheral Latin brings to me a kind of ridiculous definition. Changing the order of the names (as do many biographies) to make the best adjectived-noun phrase, I get: "Over-the-top haloed horse-loving God-speaker" and, since I don't know any German, I'm going with "son of . . . oh, nevermind" for the last name. For his name alone I'm glad he found his way into our essay today, to say nothing of his many achievements on the edge of alchemy's rebirth as chemistry, his rejection of codified medical practices in favor of experimentally verifiable methods. It is worth noting, just for the threading of this essay, that he shares a first name (and affinity for horses?) with our friend Philip Morrison, host of *The Ring of Truth*. It is also worth noting that for a long time I thought "the ring of truth" was a circular enclosure around truth, and I pictured something like the One Ring from Tolkien's classic books. So unused to and uncomfortable with ambiguity was I then.

I'm going to stop myself here, for your sake, before I get "too far out in the branches," as my wife, Karina, likes to say of my habitual method of argument, and which I find to be a beautifully apt phrase for what I like to do in my thinking and writing, and which is the way of all the great essayists, it seems to me. I could, for instance, read up a bit on the Celsus (Aulus Cornelius) whom Paracelsus considered himself "equal to or better than," or the original Theophrastus, student and successor to Aristotle, continuer of the peripatetic school of philosophy. I could research laudanum, supposedly first used medicinally by Paracelsus and certainly used inspirationally in much of the writing of Thomas De Quincey, the great-but-slightly-peripheral Romantic essayist; I could note the parallels between De Quincey's tramping about England and Paracelsus's tramping about Europe (after fleeing his post at the University of Basel in the wake of a book-burning scandal). I could read the Borges story "The Rose of Paracelsus," noting its epigraph from Thomas De Quincey—

Insolent vaunt of Paracelsus, that he would restore the original rose or violet out of the ashes settling from its combustion . . .

—and think on my long obsession with irreversible processes, and feel that I have once again stumbled upon a path long ago trod by others far greater than I, and agree that "every step you take is the goal you seek."

Alas, all essays, it occurs to me, should be gnomic, saying what they may but without persnickety certainties, which are usually conditioned and contextual anyway, and often survive well past their usefulness, as Paracelsus taught us.

Insomnia

My wife, the mother of our four children, a generally responsible woman who cares deeply for her family and tends to order and general neatness of place and of time, stayed out until almost two a.m. last night visiting our neighbors the Aguilars, whose name must mean something about tending eagles, whereas Karina's maiden name, Cabrera, has something to do with tending goats. My own last name, Madden, may derive from the Gaelic for "little dog," though my family coat of arms features a falcon seizing a duck. My son, being the fourth of a continuous line of Patrick Charles Maddens that began in 1917 with my grandfather, and being the son of a Uruguayan woman, goes by the nickname Pato, which in Spanish means duck, the animal, not the verb. In any case, the eagle would probably win in a battle with the goat, the little dog, and even with the falcon. The duck is already dead or dying, which might keep the falcon occupied while the eagle goes for the goat.

Which is to say that you can essay about anything, find some small hook in the overlooked or takenforgranted. When I was young, I read in a description of my coat of arms the phrase "falcon seizing a duck argent," which I took to mean a kind of duck or perhaps something akin to *agent*. Years later, once I'd visited Argentina (though long after I'd heard the band Argent's song "Hold Your Head Up"), I understood that *argent* was the color of both the falcon and the duck, a fancy way of saying *silver*.

The band Argent occupies the same file in my brain as the bands Bread and Free. All three float rather vaguely through my mind, which is otherwise highly ordered when it comes to rock and roll. Free I remember because one day when my junior high class went to New York for a field trip, my best friend Vin and I had some free time and so were browsing the record stacks at a shop in the Village. We thought we were funny when we found a band we'd never heard of before, saying stuff like, "Hey, this record is Free!" There were only half a dozen other people in the store, and maybe only two of them within earshot, but wouldn't you know it, one of them was a rabid Free fan. He glared at us and droned, "Hey, don't knock it." It didn't really matter that we weren't.

Argent was formed by Rod Argent, formerly of the Zombies, along with two future members of the Kinks and a guy named Russ Ballard, who wrote many of their songs. Besides the slightly repetitive "Hold Your Head Up," their other big hit—which was bigger, years later, when it was covered by KISS—was "God Gave Rock and Roll to You" (which I don't doubt).

The first record I ever owned was KISS's *Double Platinum*, which I bought at Sears, with my own money, and which my father convinced me to get instead of *Alive!* because, he said, live recordings tended to be sloppier, less precise than studio recordings. I brought the silver-sleeved LP home and played "Making Love" over and over again with no idea about what it might mean. That's not true. I thought, based on the band's name, that it meant kissing, perhaps spelled out and singsongy: "k-i-s-s-i-n-g" and all that.

My favorite KISS guy was Ace Frehley, the only one with silver makeup, whose 1977 solo album featured Ace's cover of Russ Ballard's "New York Groove." The way I figure, The Star (Paul Stanley) might be able to win in a battle against The Cat (Peter Criss), assuming it's a regular cat and not a man-sized were-cat of some kind, but neither of them would be any match for The Demon (Gene Simmons) or The Space Man (Ace). And in a battle between The Demon and The Space Man, given futuristic technology and a higher understanding of the laws of the universe, what the heck, my money's on The Space Man.

Insomnia (feat. Lina María Ferreira Cabeza-Vanegas)

My wife, the mother of our four children, a generally responsible woman who cares deeply for her family and tends to order and general neatness of place and of time, stayed out until almost two a.m. last night visiting our neighbors the Aguilars, whose name must mean something about tending eagles, whereas Karina's maiden name, Cabrera, has something to do with tending goats. My own last name, Madden, may derive from the Gaelic for "little dog," though my family coat of arms features a falcon seizing a duck. My son, being the fourth of a continuous line of Patrick Charles Maddens that began in 1917 with my grandfather, and being the son of a Uruguayan woman, goes by the nickname Pato, which in Spanish means duck, the animal, not the verb. In any case, the eagle would probably win in a battle with the goat, the little dog, and even with the falcon. The duck is already dead or dying, which might keep the falcon occupied while the eagle goes for the goat.

Which is to say that you can essay about anything, find some small hook in the overlooked or taken for granted. When I was young, I read in a description of my coat of arms the phrase "falcon seizing a duck argent," which I took to mean a kind of duck or perhaps something akin to agent. Years later, once I'd visited Argentina (though long after I'd heard the band Argent's song "Hold Your Head Up"), I understood that *argent* was the color of both the falcon and the duck, a fancy way of saying *silver*.

The band Argent occupies the same file in my brain as the bands Bread and Free. All three float rather vaguely through my mind, which is otherwise highly ordered when it comes to rock and roll. Free I remember because one day when my junior high class went to New York for a field trip, my best friend Vin and I had some free time and so were browsing the record stacks at a shop in the Village. We

21

thought we were funny when we found a band we'd never heard of before, saying stuff like, "Hey, this record is Free!" There were only half a dozen other people in the store, and maybe only two of them within earshot, but wouldn't you know it, one of them was a rabid Free fan. He glared at us and droned, "Hey, don't knock it." It didn't really matter that we weren't.

Argent was formed by Rod Argent, formed of the Zombies, along with two future members of the Kinks, and a guy named Russ Ballard, who wrote many of their songs. Besides the slightly repetitive "Hold Your Head Up," their other big hit—which was bigger, years later, when it was covered by KISS—was "God Gave Rock and Roll to You" (which I don't doubt).

The first record I ever owned was KISS's *Double Platinum*, which I bought at Sears, with n money, and which my father convinced me to get instead of *Alive!* because, he said, live recordings tended to be sloppier, less precise than studio recordings. I brought the silver-sleeved LP home and played "Making Love" over and over again with no idea about what it might mean. That's not true. I thought, based on the band's name, that it meant "kissing," perhaps spelled out and singsongy: "k-i-s-s-i-n-g" and all that.

My favorite kiss guy was Ace Frehley, the only one with silver makeup, whose 1977 solo album featured Ace's cover of Russ Ballard's "New York Groove." The way I figure, The Star (Paul Stanley) might be able to win in a battle against The Cat (Peter Criss), assuming it's a regular cat and not a man-sized were-cat of some kind, but neither of them would be any match for The Demon (Gene Simmons) or The Space Man (Ace). And in a battle between The Demon and The Space Man, given futuristic technology and a higher understanding of the laws of the universe, what the heck, my money's on the Space Man.

Unpredictable Essays

1. The world limits inclinations with each revolution.
I have learned to interpret what happens only as
I write*. There's more to live without than there
is to get inside. I have come to understand others
unclearly, sometimes halfheartedly, rarely boldly,
but I know that laughing is our common ground. And
so this is my essay of the wonders of life. Each
sentence seems its own aphorism, a particle afloat
humming in harmony with the others.

* Given my long interest in the possibilities for computers to mimic or create new texts in a writer's style (especially mine), it is perhaps no surprise that I would find Botnik's Predictive Writer (http://botnik.org/apps/writer/) utterly fascinating. Although the way it works is less magical than I had hoped, it nevertheless does make interesting sentences. I have uploaded the full text of my two books, and the software creates a predictive keyboard much like the one on a smartphone, but with twenty-eight suggestions instead of three. I "wrote" these essayistic vignettes using the computer's recommendations, selecting words that make some kind of sense together. The product is a kind of android: part human, part machine.

2. In Uruguay, where I have always found myself
awakened, unknowing, I began to believe that ideas
collaborate*. Whether the world laughs heartily
or skeletons understand the laughing, I realize
that I think more than before. So does Jerome, who
assures us that death is being, just as birds are

```
unbounded. We have always felt that existence is
a strange amorphous miracle that means everything.
Then all material against this backdrop is like a
weaver's heart: a kind of gossamer realization that
what we observe is not nature but a reassignment of
letters across town.
```

* Bakhtin, *The Dialogic Imagination*: "Language, for the individual consciousness, lies on the borderline between oneself and the other. The word in language is half someone else's. It becomes 'one's own' only when the speaker populates it with his own intention, his own accent, when he appropriates the word, adapting it to his own semantic and expressive intention. Prior to his moment of appropriation, the word does not exist in a neutral and impersonal language (it is not, after all, out of a dictionary that the speaker gets his words!), but rather it exists in other people's mouths, in other people's contexts, serving other people's intentions: it is from there that one must take the word, and make it one's own." And if the speaker is half machine? Or if the basket from which one chooses words is not quite a dictionary but a probability engine?

```
3. That was almost nothing, but even now only my mind
   will hang memories to give this essay alleyways
   of contemplation. Still I know through portals of
   subversion and decay*, indirectly, the semblance of a
   moment. Pick a day when you were contained entirely
   within two planes: the vicious and the domestic. When
   you compare yourself now to pictures of injustice,
   who were you? How can we know? From somewhere else
   the minutes recreate faulty obstacles.
```

* I first became aware of Botnik's capabilities through a Facebook-shared (perhaps "viral" is accurate) article linking to a new *Harry Potter* chapter created with the predictive keyboard. While the creators' tweet stated clearly, "We used predictive keyboards trained

on all seven books to ghostwrite this spellbinding new Harry Potter chapter," most articles that picked up the story claimed that "a bot" or "a robot" *wrote* the chapter ("and it's delightfully hilarious" said Mashable). That, I suppose, is the Holy Grail I'm searching for: a computer that can create its own Patrick Madden essays without actual input from Patrick Madden. For the time being, though, I'll chuckle along with the rest of the world at oddball Rowlingish sentences like "The tall Death Eater was wearing a shirt that said 'Hermione Has Forgotten How To Dance,' so Hermione dipped his face in mud."

I first became aware of Bakhtin in graduate school (where else?), where I read selected passages of narrative theory, understanding only vaguely the ideas his (translated) words meant to convey. I struggled with his texts, glossing over long passages but sighing with relief when I encountered an aphoristic, intelligible idea. For the time being, I chuckle along with the rest of the world at offbeat Bakhtinian sentences like "The word in living conversation is directly, blatantly, oriented toward a future answer-word: it provokes an answer, anticipates it and structures itself in the answer's direction. Forming itself in an atmosphere of the already spoken, the word is at the same time determined by that which has not yet been said but which is needed and in fact anticipated by the answering word."

I first became aware of the sonic similarities between the words *Botnik* and *Bakhtin* only now, as I write and consider the prominent names aloud. The terms are phonemic anagrams, which fact gives me a rush of delight, which is, I think, one of the purposes of literature: beyond utilitarian conveyance of information, savory artistic pleasure.

4. Variations of garlic in new connections stretch the belief that I could puzzle out my own thinking. Wednesdays postulate objects hinting toward amoebic difficulties until garlic bulbs tied with considerations gather excuses and people respond with

```
infinite divisibility. Garlic's name remains borrowed
and revealed across our arsenal of this and that
adjective from before our failing prophecy. Largely
intact, I realize things I never worried about,
resigned that I will find nothing more substantial
than the requisite emotion. *
```

* These brief essay-like paragraphs that you see here were shaped from the possibilities Botnik suggested from its analysis of my books, but I was the one choosing which of twenty-eight words to insert after each of the previous words I'd selected from a prior list of twenty-eight. This was interesting, quite often frustrating, never quite as easy as I'd hoped. "Language, whether processed by the ear or the eye, relies on a system where word follows word, line follows line, ideas accumulate through the rituals of diction" (Wendy S. Walters, "How to Fix Catastrophe"). In truth, the process was quite a bit like writing *without* a predictive keyboard, perhaps because I subconsciously tend to draw from the same word bank even without a computer mediating the process (in my two books there are 16,392 unique words out of 141,833 total; "like" is my most common "real" [nonfunction] word, with 333 occurrences, because I'm a valley girl, I suppose). Were I to load another author's works into Botnik's memory, perhaps I'd arrive at something more whimsical, like the *Harry Potter* chapter, but feeding myself my own words may have gotten me into a self-perpetuating loop.

5.
```
Perhaps transubstantiations happen all the time
with their incongruous interconnections holding
on to furniture from the fringes. Everybody loves
mystery*, at least with the spacey metaphors from
atop the tombs of local veterans. Between theory and
desire the ancients returned to give away the entire
palace of similarities between unending experiences
and divisible recoveries. Temporary poses against
their oppressive deaths.
```

    * Should these interstitial paragraphs respond to or otherwise explain the nonsense they follow? Analyze or extrapolate? Perhaps only to comment that their inanity reflects the inanity of their source texts: faux-erudite phrases jumbled together in a semblance of meaning aimed primarily at convincing the reader of the writer's intelligence . . . which is itself a form of dialogic, allowing for widely variant interpretations. George Orwell listed first of his four great motives for writing, "Sheer egoism: Desire to seem clever, to be talked about, to be remembered after death . . ." And surely, as E. B. White asserted, "Some people find the essay the last resort of the egotist, a much too self-conscious and self-serving form for their taste; they feel that it is presumptuous of a writer to assume that his little excursions or his small observations will interest the reader." Mea culpa; mea maxima culpa. But what, then, is predictive text generated from my former writings now creating new writings? Perhaps a white flag, a recognition of self-defeat.

6. Devils scream out with impotence from centuries ago: "Those mentioned in the histories haunt the capacity to make people below restrain themselves from thinking about them." Somehow this is comforting. We start with Montaigne and his small studies in life's brevity. Later we remember Cleopas* and his friend disappeared from the realm of the miracle that is possibility. A montage of fragmented notions about these darkening dangerous conventions . . . a whirling immensity exploited by an impossibility.

    * Botnik seems to have a preference for obscure words. Cleopas, one of the disciples who unknowingly encountered Jesus on the road to Emmaus, appears only once in my books, in a montage of people who saw the resurrected Lord before Thomas famously doubted. To my knowledge, Luke's gospel is the only written mention of Cleopas, as unwitting witness, one of a small number of necessary figures whose testimony made real the resurrection of a slain god.

(To make matters more interesting, Cleopas and his companion believe it their duty to inform the stranger along the road about "the things which happened [in Jerusalem]," thus recounting to Jesus the story of his crucifixion. In the account, he resists the urge to stop them, "Dudes, I *know!*") Now he is in a second book of mine, propagating almost genetically through my works, which is essentially what I am hoping for myself: that the computers of the future will discover my writing and resurrect me, take it upon themselves to write new Patrick Madden essays long after I am gone.

7. Respiration asks only to give, to make people respond, mindful of our elemental excursions, mendicants who ply our frail circumstances, holding vigil against the influence of machines*. Because time limits excuses along the day, I halfway recognize my isolation, for instance, as centuries of loss transformed into Morse code, staccato clucks holding firmly, vaguely, as if unsatisfied with our antics. The most common reminder of matter is higher indeed than the most wondrous saying (though factual).

* It occurs to me that some readers may find no discernible difference between the numbered paragraphs and their asterisked followers, so obtuse is my mind as it draws upon decades of accumulated vocabulary. And yet perhaps these disparate meldings are more than meaningless letters or sounds abutted. Consider the way the reading mind so desires meaning that it works for connections absent (or intentionless) in the text: see in the passage above the struggle for calm and meditative focus, the easy denial of the void, the incessant transformation of life into symbol. Remember that for all its beauty, language is representational; matter matters.

8. Release the idea of continuing on into these descending letters while attending to ordinary objects hinting at isolation. There are exceptions to preachings. Instead of hardcore requests dashing through portals whose struggle includes each passenger's impositions, the fastidious hand rests holding unreality. When Nero dangers forth from suburbia, marksmanship stalls temporarily and arrogance scams bearers. This situation is placated with only minor variations on imperturbability as the first mathematical principles* pass from chaos to nothing.

* In his 1903 book *Principles of Mathematics*, Bertrand Russell asserts absolute space and time (the most convenient frame of reference for physics calculations, but not the currently accepted view of physicists, or essayists, or anyone who's ever mused on time's plasticity "when you're having fun" or watching a pot boil) and discovers a paradox in set theory, the most famous example of which my father excitedly shared with me when I was a boy. He must have gotten it from Martin Gardner's column in *Scientific American*, which he subscribed to and read steadily during my entire childhood. "The Barber Paradox" goes: Suppose there is a

barber who shaves all the men in town who do not shave themselves and only those men who do not shave themselves. Can this barber shave himself? Russell himself extrapolates it thusly:

"You can define the barber as 'one who shaves all those, and those only, who do not shave themselves.' The question is, does the barber shave himself? . . . I think it is clear that you can only get around it by observing that the whole question of whether a class is or is not a member of itself is nonsense, i.e., that no class either is or is not a member of itself, and that it is not even true to say that, because the whole form of words is just noise without meaning."

9. Likewise the idea of completeness: from insights to music I never made, I construct a series of pages around the idea of mirrors. What paralytic reasoning to make something matter! Enough about mimics! My grandmother sang away her ills that you might remember to make possible the gists of everything. Either way, we can believe that the expanding universe babbles on toward its own ephemeral patterns*.

* As, I hope, does this essay . . . inevitably? Perhaps the set of words without meaning, or combinations of words that mean nothing, is a null set, or it contains an inherent contradiction, because, to take an extreme example, a lecture in, say, Japanese will seem "noise without meaning" *to me*, yet I cannot say that it *has* no meaning. Similarly, even Borges's maddeningly hypothetical infinite books in the Library of Babel may *mean* to particular readers, or, in sum, in the abstract, they certainly *mean* (in a multiversally metaphorical garden-of-forking-paths kind of way) even to me. For what it's worth, Botnik offered me "bubbles" above, after "universe," and I chose it, but later, in revision, after hitting upon Borges—who himself was alluding to the Bible story explaining the division of languages—and noting the phonemic (if not etymological) similarities between "Babel" and "babble," I changed the vowel. So what?/So there.

10. But perhaps the matter is analogous to the ascension of laughter to the sky. From elysian fields to transient beaches, I lament the proof of genre, longing for variety (or stability). Tunnels represent falling slowly into seemingly unimportant gibberish, but everything regarding negative capability appears ironic, partly because of joys and partly because of consternations. Who said it was meant to be so imitative? Name one disillusioned nineteenth-century German and flip the world*. Whispering does this, changes existing legends while increasing dependence on dubious destiny.

* Nietzsche, *Human, All Too Human*: "We really suppose that in language we possess a knowledge of the cosmos," yet (he suggests) language as a structure of consciousness is both the way we apprehend the world and the way we create it. This essay, which began as a frivolous exercise, has become, for me at least, a kind of engine, humming in harmony with itself, self-perpetuating and self-actualizing. I say this not to suggest that the essay drives itself, but that the essay and I are symbiotic, as I both write and read it into meaning. Someday (*now*; the essay exists in the perpetual now), you will read it, too, and it will mean again, but differently. As Andrei Linde said, "It's not enough for information to be stored somewhere, completely inaccessible to anybody. It's necessary for somebody to look at it. You need an observer who looks at the universe. In the absence of observers, our universe is dead." Yet I also feel as if this particular selection and ordering of doubly preexisting words has achieved its own momentum, so that, with barely a nudge from me, it continues accumulating and meaning, potential energy becoming a reality, not *reality* writ firm, but one version of it, your reality, the part that is a contextualization and interpretation of these words I've committed to electronic paper and transmitted over the ether to other media to bring them to

you, so that you may *realize* them. Your witness *makes real* these words and in effect transports, even (in a small way) *resurrects*, me.

This android essay reminds us that we are participants in the creation of the universe, that our observations are necessary to the resolution of possibility into actuality, that, in the words of Alan Watts, "We are the witnesses through which the universe becomes conscious of its glory, of its magnificence."

Laughter (feat. Jericho Parms)

As for insight into character, perhaps there is no better tell than what we laugh at. My wife, Karina, and I coincide on large swaths of the humorous, but we lean toward particular ends of the spectrum, which sometimes leads to confused looks and shaken heads. For me, the most risible moments are mostly about puns, the snatches of insight made possible by the imprecisions and overlappings of language. I've had a number of hearty linguistic laughs in my life, but none, I think, so sublime as this, the one time I truly (and unselfconsciously) fell and rolled on the floor laughing.

One of the games my family likes to play is Balderdash, in which contestants attempt to create credible definitions of odd words to fool their friends. For instance, you might get *hinnable*, which might mean A) "preposterous and illogical" or B) "capable of being harvested numerous times in one year" or C) "able to neigh or whinny." Did you guess C? If you did, you get two points. If not, you've earned me or Karina a point. Typically, you're choosing from a half dozen or more humorously plausible definitions to words like *omphaloskepsis* ("gazing at one's navel while meditating") and *gongoozler* ("a lazy, good for nothing person") and *crotaline* ("pertaining to rattlesnakes"), so your chances of winning are firmly probabilistic, though it never seems to matter who comes out on top, as long as everybody has a good laugh along the way.

Sometime in the early nineties, Parker Brothers expanded the game to include four additional bluffing categories: People (wherein you must guess why they're noteworthy), Initials (supply the words behind the acronym), Movies (give the basic plot), and Dates (tell what important event happened then). They called the result Beyond Balderdash. This is the version that Karina and I own.

One day when my parents were visiting us in Ohio, we broke out the game to enliven our evening. As usual, I was winning, not because

I knew any of the clues (the only Balderdash word I've ever actually known was *funambulator*), but because I could often sense (and imitate) the writing style of the game designer. But as I've said, winning didn't matter, and we were enjoying the repartee. Nobody was sure what had happened on 3/26/37, but someone suggested that that was when FDR signed social security into law. The movie *Take It Big* may have featured a British soldier in India who kidnaps an elephant to win the heart of a local beauty. The RCRA, according to the card, *really* stands for Refrigeration Compressor Rebuilders Association, but I preferred my father's "Resource Conservation and Recovery Act" (as does all-acronyms.com, and a Google search produces *ten thousand times* as many hits for the latter). In any case, my point, before getting to my real point, is that in a world where even a quark's velocity and position are uncertain, who can really know such trivia?

Then, as things were winding up, it was my turn to act as reader, so I collected everybody's definitions for *pahoehoe*, a word, it turns out, that means hardened basaltic lava forming smooth undulations. I hid the scraps of paper inside the box top and arranged them so I could read without giving anything away, but before I could clear my throat, my eyes alighted on my father's mistake; instead of a definition, he had written an *acronymic expansion* for the term:

Put A Hat On Elderly Heroes Of Europe

I fell sideways out of my chair to the floor, grabbed my gut, juddered uncontrollably. My eyes welled up, my throat blurted out whinnies and whines, I could not get a breath in edgewise. Although they couldn't know what had caused the paroxysm, my family, first tentatively, then wholeheartedly, joined in the chorus, and we laughed all together for a long while, until I composed myself, then explained amidst breakouts of new laughter, then we laughed again when we all understood the joke of my father's misunderstanding. For hours, it seems now, the smooth undulations of sound rippled off the walls and reverberated through the apartment, out into the street, filling the town with merriment and hope.

With the aid of an ultrasound, a baby's heartbeat sounds like 1)
a hovering chopper, 2) a fast-moving train, 3) a snicker or prayer.
Upon first hearing the sound, my body, then only ten weeks preg-
nant, erupted into a bout of ungovernable, uncharacteristically
high-pitched laughter, a howl so unexpected that my Doppler-
wielding midwife couldn't pull the device away in time, capturing
and amplifying my laughter into a roar. This startled me into an
even harder laugh that nearly rocked me off the table, inspiring my
husband to break up and a nearby nurse to chortle at our delight.
Holding my breath, I composed myself long enough for the midwife
to count 160 heartbeats. BPM of course stands for "Beats Per Min-
ute," but it could just as easily suggest

Beerbohm Put It Mildly

when he wrote that he preferred laughter take him unaware—"only
so can it master and dissolve me." Who knows what happened on
3/26/37, but on that date some eighty years later what had been the
source of my greatest crack up—a beat ricocheting in my belly—
became a child in flesh: birthed and named, inserting itself, claiming
space no one imagined with its own style and cadence. What bold
intrusion! What intimate trespass! Yet if intimacy is meant to be
shared, laughter seems the best device, dissolving us all, forgoing the
status quo for the clumsy interpretations of others, for the pureness of
hysteria or unsullied relief, for the allowance of joy.

For Karina, on the other hand, slapstick is king, and I have never seen
her laugh as hard or as long (she is still laughing today, whenever she
recalls the image, even now, as she reads over my shoulder) as the
time Eduardo Cariello snuck in late to church, during the opening
hymn, dressed smartly in his suit in preparation to give a talk on some
serious point of doctrine. He found an empty spot in the congrega-
tion and gingerly placed his briefcase on the last folding chair in the
row, casting about brief looks of apology and mouthing the words
of the hymn. Karina and I, sitting and singing a scant distance away,
noted with wry smiles the uncomfortable position our Uruguayan

friend found himself in, and then, just as we intoned the triumphal conclusion to Charles Wesley's "Come, Let Us Anew"—"Enter into my joy and sit down on my throne" [not really, but that would have been cool]—he sat. But not on a chair. With one hand still holding the handle of his bag, he crashed to the floor, where there never was a chair, then tumbled backward, legs splayed, patent leather shoes wagging, neck cricked and arms waving, jacket flapped open beside his prominent brown-pinstriped rump. He righted himself right away, looked around sheepishly, made a show of dusting off, and kept right on mouthing the chorus.

Most people seemed not to notice, but Karina left immediately to snicker in the hallway, then, when all efforts to suppress her laugh failed, she stepped outside for a wholehearted guffaw. She repeated this concession to her baser nature every few minutes during the rest of the hour. When it was his turn to speak to us, Brother Cariello smiled and shook his head, apologized for his embarrassing display, then launched into his lesson. Stuck with that image of the poor man sprawled on the floor, heels over head, hind in the air, and unable to concentrate on his words, Karina and I missed his message that day. Or perhaps we didn't.

Order

Life doesn't always happen in the best order or with the best details for a story. Fiction writers can simply rearrange and embellish to craft the story they want. For a truth-teller essayist, this is not an option, unless the essayist indicates clearly the manipulations and perhaps offers them to the contemplative reader as fodder for a rumination on the nature of truth or reality or the essay genre.

First, as is always seemly, background: My wife, Karina, is from Uruguay, and her parents and siblings still live there. Our young family included Karina and me, plus four children, who ranged in age from three months to seven years at the time of our last trip down south to visit. In this particular moment, we were returning to the United States from Uruguay on New Year's, which is a Holy Day of Obligation celebrating the circumcision of Jesus.

The other piece of background information that you need to know is that my brother Dan's friend at Notre Dame made up a thing whereby you save yourself from a dead-end story you're telling, where you can see your listeners' eyes glazing, beginning to roll, by capping it off with "and then I found twenty bucks." This makes it a good, happy story. Feel free to use it. Spread the word.

So, the story: The crotchety priest in front of us on the plane from MVD to GRU repeatedly hit his flight attendant button, on and off, again and again (ping! Ping! PING! [the sound doesn't really increase in volume or intensity, but it *felt* like it did]), near the end of the flight because we were passing through turbulent air, the plane was pitching and jumping chaotically, and they wouldn't turn off the fasten-seatbelt light. The flight attendants were strapped into their pull-down seats two rows back, near the galley, so they saw him throwing his tantrum and explained, loud enough so he could hear them: "Sir, we are unable to tend to you now. Please discontinue the pressing of the button."

He glared over his shoulder and shouted, in his rudest, insultingest voice: "Then when can I go to the bathroom!?" He said this in Spanish, with that grating last-two-syllable whine that Uruguayans affect overmuch and without thinking. I wanted to smack him in the back of the head and knock his glasses off. I restrained myself.

When we got off the plane in Rio de Janeiro, Karina and I grabbed the kids and our carry-on bags. It was Daniela sitting comfortably in a frontpack with Karina; Sara struggling in my arms, trying to get down, hanging out away from me; Pato complaining about tugging the rolling mini-suitcase; Adi slinging a backpack; Karina and I carrying the four other unwieldy bags. I want you to get the picture: Two parents, four small tired children, six bags precariously slung and dangling and rolling.

From one plane to the next, we had to walk down several long signless corridors, then ride up an elevator, to a snaking roped-off security line where, eventually, we had to unload everything on a conveyor belt, take off our shoes and jackets, and walk through a metal detector, taking care to keep Sara from running away when I put her down. As we got off the elevator, Father Cantankerous, who was behind us, brusquely shoved his way past, knocking Karina and three-month-old Daniela sideways, to get in the security line before us.

I was seething, sending all sorts of bad vibes his way, imagining myself sweeping his legs to take him down.

Earlier, when we were still on the plane and the clenching cleric was fighting to keep his bowels under control, the stewardesses finally gave in: "You can get up, but we can't be responsible if anything happens to you." He harrumphed, and I think he gave them the evil eye as he turned past them to push open the folding door. Right then I decided I had to get Sara's diaper changed. I laid her on the seat next to me. She was invisible to the people in the last row of the plane, between me and the bathroom. When I managed to get the diaper off, it was the nasal equivalent of deafening. I turned my head and fluttered my eyes. It took 3.5 wipes to get rid of that caked-on mess, but finally, just as Father Impatient snapped open the door, I got her suited back up.

Later that day, as we waited for our next plane and chased our children, Karina told me that the couple in the row behind us, backs to the bathroom, were commenting on the horrific smell, thinking it was the priest in the toilet. Ah, sweet, putrid, displaced justice.

Then, as we labored with our shoes and slippery children and cumbersome bags, as we watched the unburdened reverend saunter away, Karina thought she saw something under the X-ray machine exit belt. She whispered to Pato, "Go under there and pick that up." He was uncooperative, grumbling something about fine, then he's not taking the suitcase anymore. "Go *under* there and pick that *up*." What do you know: we'd found twenty bucks. Times two, it turned out. We looked around cursorily to offer the Jacksons to whomever might be searching for them, but, unsuccessful at that, we stuffed them in our pockets, Karina and I, then veritably skipped a few yards down the inevitable path and bought some Brazilian chocolates in the Duty Free Shop.

Memorizing the Lyrics

> Verses and snatches of these ballads are continually haunting and twittering about my memory, as in summer the swallows haunt and twitter about the eaves of my dwelling. I know them so well, and they meet a mortal man's experience so fully, that I am sure . . . I could conduct the whole of my business by quotation.
>
> —ALEXANDER SMITH, "A Shelf in My Bookcase"

Slowly, over the course of a dozen years or so, it has dawned on me that, for all my talk, I'm not truly living up to the essayistic ideals. Week after week, semester after semester, I preach to my students the virtues of idleness and contemplation, curiosity and attention, yet aside from those seventy-five-minute respites carved into the day, I'm frantic with work. It's good work, mostly, and almost entirely of my own choosing, so I feel inclined to chant, with Joe Walsh, "I can't complain, but sometimes I still do. Life's been good to me so far." Yet I also feel to explain that I'm not always or not only complaining. I'm chiding myself, seeking self-restitution and an end to my hypocrisy.

My leisure shortcoming, particularly, came singing into my mind again recently, when I returned from a business trip to find my last, lately arrived Christmas gift from Karina: the new double CD from La Vela Puerca, called *Piel y Hueso* ("skin and bone"; don't ask me to translate the band name; okay, if you insist: it's something like "the pig candle," which I suspect is a reference to a marijuana joint, but I'm not sure, having cultivated since high school a persona that's blissfully ignorant of such things). I had been wanting the CD ever since I discovered its existence just before the holidays, and even before then I'd hoped for some new songs, but as an import from South America, the disc had taken its sweet time. You might want to know that La Vela Puerca is a Uruguayan band formed around the turn of the century consisting of eight members on guitars, bass, drums, trumpet, saxophone, and vocals. They perform a lively mixture of rock and ska (often with a touch of murga) with emotive lyrics that highlight the economic difficulties in their home country and sympathize with (and give wings to) the melancholic dreamer. What's more, they represent, to me, a sudden surge of originality in Uruguayan music, after some dreary times in the eighties and nineties, which were full of derivative songs echoing the worst of Brit keyboard pop.

The next day, I loaded the CD onto my computer so I could have its songs on my iPod so I could listen to it during my commute, as I typically do with new CDs. But instead of then filing the case in its alphabetical spot on my shelves, I carried it with me for several days, suddenly ashamed at how I'd been treating music lately. Time was, half a lifetime ago, when I would sit for hours, playing records on my turntable, singing along to the words written on the paper sleeves. How I studied those stanzas, absorbing the rhymes, becoming the stories and lessons they taught. How I relished the solitude, the focused attention to the frivolous task of memorizing the lyrics. For a kid raised in the 1970s and '80s in suburban New Jersey, this was as close as I got to meditation, and as for the knowledge I gained and ideas I absorbed (from Rush lyrics, in large part, but also Beatles and Steely Dan and Yes and Toad the Wet Sprocket and so many more): I feel today that they are priceless.

For instance? Well, independence of thought, or at least a kind of skeptical consciousness of the forces that seek to manipulate us for profit. ("His mind if not for rent . . . ," etc.) Maybe a love of literature, too, as I've detailed elsewhere, from discovering the allusive portals from Rush songs to great works of literature. Even an advanced "theory of mind," a recognition that others thought and felt just as I did, though often differently, which grew, I believe, into empathy for the less fortunate, or differently fortunate.

I am sure that some people a generation or more ahead of me disdained my idleness, derided my decision to sit rapt with my music as trivial and wasteful, just as I consider my son's enthusiasm for video games to be detrimental. But not so long ago, parents and preachers kept their children away from books, novels especially, on the grounds that they would stifle the imagination and inspire rebellion, whereas now we have research to suggest that reading literature creates compassion. In the lowerarchy of vices, listening to records can't really be that bad.

In any case, lately I realized that I'd turned my back on this formative activity, traded it for mindless Internet surfing or (sometimes, more rarely) sitcom watching. True, my life was now rife with productive busyness, too, and so many activities derived from loving my large family, shrinking my available time, yet there was no denying that I was shirking my self-restorative duty here. With my enthusiasm for La Vela Puerca's new album, I sought to make a conscious course correction.

More than anybody I know, more than anybody I've met, I am a kind of jukebox, always ready to burst forth into song suggested by an offhand comment in casual conversation. Nearly every time I see a white car drive by, my mind goes straight to Yes's "White Car" "mov[ing] like a ghost on the skyline." Sometimes, when I'm in polite company, I sing only in my mind, but if I am alone or feel confident among my companions, I'll sing right out loud. Take a recent game night with my friends, for example. Brad mentions the game clock "ticking away," so I sing, "Ticking away the moments that make up the dull day." Travis divides the different colored blocks, so I chant, "You gotta keep 'em separated." Kelly wonders aloud whether a character is immune to flies, and I melodize with "You like to think that you're immune to the stuff, oh yeah!" Juan gets up to refill his cup, walking around the kitchen island because he's blocked from the shortest route, and I intone, "Take the long way home." Mark finishes his turn and nods in my direction, "You're up," so I burst out with "It's the final countdown!"

When my brother Dan and I worked together one summer, temp-secretarying at Exxon, we spent hours each day emailing each other one-liners from song lyrics in quick succession, each addition a suggestion from the previous:

> . . . where I was born lived a man who sailed the sea
> Crown thy good with brotherhood from sea to shining sea

I'm sailing away, set an open course for the virgin sea
Sailing takes me away to where I always doo dat da dee
De do do do, de da da da is all I want to say to you
All I want is to feel this way, to be this close, to feel the same
All I wanna do is have some fun. I've got a feeling I'm not the only one
You're the one that I want, you're the only one I want
I want you. I want you so bad
I'm bad, I'm bad, jam on
We jammin'. I want to jam it with you
I can't live with or without you
Life goes on within you and without you
Obladi oblada, life goes on, brah!
Life is what happens to you while you're busy making other plans
Oh life, is bigger, it's bigger than you, and you are not me

You can take it from here (the exchange my brother copied and pasted into an email to me apparently took place entirely on Friday, June 20, 2000, and goes on for five single-spaced pages of one-liners, ending with [you guessed it] "Stairway to Heaven").

And on our commutes to and fro, we played "the radio game," quick-changing through the preset stations, one point for the song name, one for the band. I dominated the "oldies" while Dan killed me on the modern stuff. We rarely spent more than a second guessing.

Given my music-dedicated past, I felt my self-betrayal acutely. When had I gotten too busy to give my full attention to music? When had music become for me just background, something to do while I was engaged in more directly marketable actions? I was rightly ashamed. It had been so long since I'd sat down just to listen to music. And I guess I missed that, or I missed the life I had then that let me do such a thing, or I missed the person I was, who could balance his life in such a way as to allow time to just sit and sing.

With such inclinations in my heart I went to my closet yesterday in the evening, and resolved to memorize some lyrics from my new record. Given that the album contains eighteen songs, and the writers are relatively verbose (no I-wanna-rock-and-roll-all-night repetitions here), I decided to start small, with the song I liked best, "Sé a donde quiere ir," or "I know where she wants to go," with its melancholic/hopeful/purposeful theme:

Salió de casa y tras de si	She left her home and closed the door
Dejó sus miedos	on all her fears
Y con el frío que sintió	And with a blast of icy air
Lloró de nuevo	returned her tears
Ya ves	You see?
Al caminar se tropezó	On her way she ran right
Con mi desvelo	Into my awakening
Y allí la tuve que abrazar	Right there I caught her in my arms
Bajo mi cielo	Below the darkening
Ya ves	Sky
A dónde quiere ir	Where will she go
Si no la quieren ver	If no one really cares?

I sat cross-legged on the floor with the CD booklet balanced between my fingers and listened to the song on repeat, singing along, feeling the movement, seeing the unfolding story, worrying then relieving, reliving the perhaps invented story of a pair of faraway strangers whose chance encounter determines the course of their lives (they seem to fall in love, but even if not, he seems to give her hope, meaning, a purpose). But I couldn't shake the intentionality of it all. I was *trying* to memorize the lyrics, and this realization sullied the enterprise, perhaps even stymied it, though eventually (not that day, but a day soon after), I achieved my goal: I had the whole song memorized, at least enough to sing along while it was playing (if not to recite it *a cappella*).

So what is this, then? Some moral victory? A return to normalcy? A calm I can recur to amidst the chaos? An overcoming of the natural man inclined to industriousness?

None of the above.

Yet never do I wholly give up the struggle, and in my heart I cherish an ideal.
—ELISABETH WOODBRIDGE MORRIS, "The Tyranny of Things"

It feels, or I feel, ambiguous. Equivocal. Unclear. Disparate. Somewhat satisfied to have recovered a semblance of my untroubled youth, yet reaffirmed in my belief that I can never get it back. Too aware, too intentional, have I become.

God help thee, Elia, how art thou changed! Thou art sophisticated.
—CHARLES LAMB, "New Year's Eve"

When we began this essay, I'd recently acquired La Vela Puerca's new CD and had committed one of its songs to memory. How goes the experiment, lo these many months later? La Vela has released yet more songs, an EP's worth, from their website, for free. I've listened through them a few times, but, as they don't quite strike my fancy as their predecessors did, I've taken no pains to sing along. But another favorite band, with, it strikes me now, a name resonant with the other's and similarly inscrutable, has also shared with the world new songs, two of them, free for those who paid for their previous album, and I've been gleefully listening, singing, and memorizing one of those. This is Toad the Wet Sprocket with "Architect of the Ruin" and "So Long, Sunny," the first of which I particularly enjoy, despite, or perhaps because of, the deep melancholy of its lyrics, which take their referent from the real-life midlife struggle and despair of Glen Phillips, the band's singer, who is approximately my age, and whose life I've often felt mirrors my own in tangential ways.

I was belting it out just this morning with the spiders and the detritus in my rickety old car on the way into work.

Repast

```
R N J X L N N M L B Y J B M B L N J B Q G Z Y Q G
T H E Z N A D M X R Y M Y G Q R D Z D J W R R M K
Z V S U O E N A R O P M E T X E R Q L T O T A H T
T H I N G S W D F Y L B Z T S A P E R T N W R G L
R M D L T E E N O N E Y A I M T N M C K H E C M V
P A G R J H L R R B M N D A O N R N Y E Z O M B R
Y T J Y G K E I E W D O D Z O I U T N Z U V G O T
J N Z Y L N K T Z W O E T Y T F Z B Z L T K R P M
W T J M J J I Q T A J R L K R G M L D Q V M M S M
T T Y T M M Y R N N B E D E W T J N T R B E T O X
J B J D K P W Y J J T E P S K R T B L Y T I T A L
X M Y N A T M R J A J X T B V K I M D T L H L X P
T T K S J E D G M E E O T H M A D T A L E T Z X G
S I M P L Y R I Q X R W M Y K E S K E R B K V Y M
I W T E T B T L Y P E L R G E P T O D R C Y W M R
L Y D A V L T O A E H M I X J S D B L A S F Z B X
M D R K U S F T N C T Y P K J M X D M E A V L D D
U Q N O M D D O L T X E D R E A D E D M M M S E Z
C D J I M N B U T A C M E X G L H Q I L K N W A T
H W N T F E I Z K T I U O A V T Y L O B Q O I H W
R T L R T I M N E I L V N R B D Y N Y N L L I T V
H A D B M R D D J O Q B O J E S C B D L Y S W L Y
N R N M K F Z N G N X P T J N E D Q A Y D L D B Z
G Q K N J Y K Y W S X Z E J N B K J J D R R Y Y Y
D I V B B Y J B N R W J D Y R Y G Q N P G Y N M G
```

At
the
repast
things
were
allowed
to
be
jovial
once
more.
Too
much
solemnity

already
that
day.
Still
there
came
a
moment
when
I
was
expected
to
speak

in
memory
of
my
mother.
I
had
dreaded
this.
I
noted
my
friends'
and

family's
likely
expectations
for
the
writer's
extemporaneous
eulogy,
and
I
made
a
perfunctory
attempt

to
speak,
but
ultimately
I
simply
couldn't
find
the
words.

```
V N Q A Y Y T P Y O A Y Y Q Y A Y X K M D W P L N
P I Y L G L Z H N M S V M R T V Z Q T Q K N N R K
T A B I B Y I C E G M N S E R A H S E F O D E L B
O G T C T G E R N J F Z W E T T K Z C J L P T Z X
T A R E N J N I A O N K E S H J J J N X A Y R N B
S J E X R Q C I B S L S S T B T Y X O S D B N G T
A Z D K R A Z T E M S I U X Y K S Y T D W K W J B
P Q U L R R P F A B M E A O S M L A O N P D T T D
I N N T Q K A P U H T Q C G L L O N P T R J D V N
T Y D M T Y S D A N W T N E A U R L R L B T Y T L
N H A Q S D T X T V E I W R N U C E O Y Q R H Z D
A G N Y A Z U J R P R R E H T R P A M G L E M B M
J U C A E T R T Z E D N A E O A T T R N I P Y Z D
M O Y M F F E K B P E K R L S R X T R I L E M X Z
T R R Y R R O M P G K R A T S A P H Q R M D S I J
H H R E O J E R R T K L E J D N T U Z L E K S R S
E T S F F M P T E D C M G P R L J S B X G T L T Z
Y Y A J E E A Q B N H A V I A E A T I N G L F M N
T N W R G H R O O T S Q Y N N S O P B G R T M A T
I R D J W G D S I Q T I J T R Q T T N P N R B Y D
M K R B Y D L W N N X A C E P N I T A L T D R O W
E J G M J M B U T R N G R R V Y B N R D O W C V A
B B R E D Z Y J M D Z V L N L N N B B K N A Y W K
W M T R R P R L Q T Y J Z A R J N G V P N L T W X
B J T D L A K T J X W V Q L M M J X L D P N L J M
```

The word *repast* shares a Latin root with pasta, antipasto, pasture, and thus refers simply to the act of eating, generally. A repast is a feast, not necessarily after a funeral. But etymologies being what they are, forensic re-memberings, tracings through time, who can miss the internal redundancy of re-past: a past once again, a miraculous return to/ of what once was.

```
M A N O T E S H T I W P D P N G Y G T Z J T Z Q Y B
V N Y W V T N N W J N J J Q T S D I M A K P B E M R
R X T K Z D J N I W K M G L N G J T P S P Y A Y B N
Y I B X W N T T N E L O D N I T R Y E E B R W T T Z
L O N X V I M D W A S T E S G D E D N L S H L P J N
G U Z L M S G D M R Y V N M C L N T D Z E G D M G L
X S Q E D D T I M E Y N N T L R E I R R T P D J D X
L L E M L R J R Y J G L M O P R O Q F Q D L Y E Q S
N Y T E B O V Q L X N L W P T N T S N M R R C K S Q
E A A T L W B L K R T I Q A N H N G S Q B O E E D Y
T T L B G B D S T O N E I R E A D L X W R Q L T N N
T O U J Z M M M M G N N H T I W W L P A O M Z A A I
I P C D P B Q U K R M L Y T W W L Z T T R R M B N L
R D L N D M S L J E I N X X L M W E J A K W D L P R
W D A A G E P U N O X R J D L L D Z H N W T T K T N
D Q C M S M W T L D D S P E L T J N J Y O G X J M B
N L T U J M S O E T H D H M D E L R A L T H O U G H
A D A R B J W G R E I T O L P E H O B D Y Q G L N R
H C L E N Z A O N D T M Z F I Y R T N E D K Z D T T
D G L H V G M L L A S N A S D S E O Y Y H Z J F E P
N O I R N O S A L L Z E U T K M H F F N M I E W X Y
U O T E T U T C D K E R A M E Y T A I T Y L N R G V
O D S H D N O G V Y E Y Y R W L A L R N E Y P D T V
F J E O E V W A S L N B R Z C E F R T E D N Y L R R
Y R K M E T L M J P P J J A H H M M Y L D X V M R Z
B U Y Q M W Y N Q R L W L S L N B B P R K V L Z Y L
```

Although	leisure	find	behind	find
she	time	words	in	a
was	to	amidst	the	yellow
often	read	the	alcove	and
anxiously	or,	jumble:	she	yellowing
engaged	in	harmless,	shared	Ultimate
in	later	indolent	with	Wordsearch
many	years,	mental	my	decorated
good	do	entertainments,	father,	with
causes,	the	wastes	atop	her
my	crossword,	of	her	handwritten
mother	calculate	time.	desk,	notes.
still	Sudoku,	Left	we	
found				

```
O O S B Y Y N L M L K T M B Q Z R D K C X T L X B B
H R E J M B E R T V R G W G Y M Z Z A O M L T M O W
T T U N R T D D P Q N T P R D Z R C M N A T L R V L
I H G S M V D T N D D L E L Y D O Y B T Y M G A V Q
M O A B E L I Q R N B V N Q D P Y A T A Y E L V P J
E G E M F G H M J A O N O Q H N N Z D I S R A N M G
T R L O Z D A Y J C N T P O Q T Y Z J N V R E X L T
H A I B R Y N U S Y T S N N W O N K N U I S J V H K
Y P N L Z R T I G T T I L D N M R Q Q A Q T N A E A
P H D N G A D N S N E S G A S E R U T C U R T S T J
Y I O T N R R X Y S A G I V T M S I E Y W A K V Y Z
R C L R I B I T M J L L L H N E O E L N Z Y E L R K
A A E E T I D S B J N T Y X P N D R D L I R B B L M
M L N A I L V L O M T J I R S E D T F U Y G K Y Y Z
I V C S A T D D L L P D P M N R R M H R L T A L T N
D E E U W S E N S E L E S S A R B M G O P C H M N Y
S R B R A D D W T A M T R P G G E N I O U C N Y I G
J B Y E M M W B T M O H N J K V I V J T U G B I I R
W A S S E R P X E I D A Y Y I H D N E S T R H V N T
S L N E D D A M N D S T O F T N T O E E Q E E T L I
J E D L U O W J N S I N Y Y L W E H R D H N D M Y S
Q K V A L L J W L T W T R M L L O V E M B T D P Y J
R Z L L X P O Z Z Z N E O J L L A R E Y A O R S B T
Q X M T E N G R D E V T D T J T K Z D J B N T T I W
T P L Q K S W Q W E R J L B N Y B L R S Y E T T P L
Y W J D J G Y T M G R N V M D I T K W B M B L J K W
```

From his indolence, Borges imagined a "Library [that] includes all verbal structures, all variations permitted by the twenty-five orthographical symbols." Such a system would contain, amidst "leagues of senseless cacophonies," "all that it is given to express, in all languages." Imagine the hidden treasures of wisdom, everything ever known or unknown, every stray thought, even our very selves, translated into dormant words awaiting discovery.

```
D Y L D M T W T I L O V E Y O U M O M K M W H W H O L
E R E M E M B E R E D L A T N E D I C C A R O Y N N K
S A S B D H W L V M Y V X E M D M L K T G O P J N M D
U R K G E R I Y M E Y S T H M G A M Q Z Z T E E O L L
N B O R R V D M R T N B R T P C Y Z B E T E V T M Y P
T I O H E B N B Z E L D J E A D N A R Y G E H T Y Y L
C L B S T P I T S R P I N I T N G O R A R E Y M I V M
E T D K Z O F H A P Z A S J I I M B L Q R B A Y S J W
T O W L Y J B E Y N A I S A Y D R L S E S I M O R P R
E G L A D D E N E D D H G S Q A I W N M X E X D F D L
R E S D T Y N B M A J A R R P M M M V T G L G P B N L
A T J P V Z A T R D R Z O E A I N T E N D E D R Y B G
P H O W A S B A D J J D R U P Y L L A U T X E T O E N
N E Y U R H P D P E T Y F N N E Q K T N Y B H X L B T
E R N N R D R E H T T R R Z D N D N D R Y U R R Z G K
H B O O K S T E G N Y U K U P R O I R P S D B J B L L
W B Y T R X S M P X L B T B M T W T S D P Y Z P V J Z
M T N B L W A L D R K I R I E N L T X C T H A N B N W
R Q B B Q M V Z E L L Q R S T M I M Z V E J Y B W T Q
L J D X E Y Y C J O Q A R M L S O T H I S R E N D W P
V N R G E C O T S D N M N P P R N R N N T P N N R K T
S D P H Q V O V T D J R P A P B Y O F L Q N P E V J W
D M T R E M G M B G Z Q W R N L P B C Z Y Y A Y D P T
R B D R E Y N Q E D Q X R Y L D R W Y E D L T G N D M
O L E I W Y B X R T P J J K K R M Q W D R R P G E X D
W D D B M J B X N K P F N Q Z M X Y X J D L L J D L B
Y Y X X Z Z N M N B R I I X T B J Y M R B G Q V D Z E
```

If,
as
Borges
promises,
"when
writers
die
they
become
books,"
then
perhaps
even
my

mother,
who
never
wrote
more
than
notes,
may
yet
be
recovered
in
my
books,

or
perhaps
discerned
and
remembered,
reconstituted
textually,
from
the
vast
gallimaufry
of
words,
both

intended
and
accidental,
and
thus
I
may
repass
our
lives
together
and
find
her

again
in
the
paradisiacal
Library.
My
solitude
is
gladdened
by
this
elegant
hope.

Happiness (feat. Amy Leach)

A more diligent essayist than I might research and catalog numerous and various last words, searching for patterns of meaning and wisdom from departed sages, but I am interested only in two. The one that set my mind thinking toward finding this essay is from Gerard Manley Hopkins, a poet I've long admired from a safe distance, which is to say that I'd never probed into his life, nor even sought his poems, though I've been moved by their sprung rhythms when they've crossed my path, in classes and so forth. So who knows why I found myself on Wikipedia reading up on the man? Actually, in writing that last sentence, which was honest when I began it, I have recovered my memory a bit: I had been reading piecemeal in Nick Ripatrazone's 2013 book on Catholic literature, *The Fine Delight*, primarily because Nick and I grew up in the same small town of Whippany, New Jersey, and secondarily because Nick had deigned to quote me a wee bit in his work. There I found some probing passages on Hopkins, learned that he'd been a Jesuit priest, perhaps that he'd died before publishing a word, a detail that never fails to confound/impress an ambitious word-peddler like myself, so I sought to round out my knowledge, which I did, discovering his battles with depression, his melancholic life in Ireland, away from his English home, his dilemma between humility and publishing, and his young death from typhoid fever. On his death bed, his biographer reports, he exclaimed, "I am so happy, I am so happy. I loved my life," which our anonymous Wikipedia editor pits in curious opposition to the other evidences.

I felt glad for him, and I believed his last judgment, just as I believe William Hazlitt, who, in conditions quite different from Hopkins's vow-directed asceticism, seems also to have led an unhappy life: failure as a painter, unhappy romances, quarrels with friends, disappointed ideals, ridicule from literary peers, compounded by sickness and pain that led him, too, to an early death. Also like Hopkins, Hazlitt's self-assessment in his last moments was a surprise: "Well, I've had a happy life,"* he said to his son and a small group of friends as he expired. Knowing something of humors, as involved and distant observer both, I understand that the final assessment may be skewed by a mood or a wish to be remembered well or even by some deep comprehension to which the still-living have no access. Yet in the naïve hope available only to the still-living, I agree with Montaigne, that we should not judge of our happiness until after our death, or at its arrival, at least.

* *In that one old story, one servant received five talents from his master, invested them, ended up with ten talents, and finally entered into joy. Another servant only got one talent, and he kept it in a napkin for safekeeping, and finally entered into outer darkness. Perhaps the ten-talent fellow had an otherwise sad and painful life, while the napkin man had a sweet and easy life. Still, whether they had used their talents or not determined whether they finally entered into joy or darkness. "We totter on the brink of nothing," wrote William Hazlitt. To have tottered on the brink of nothing but to have written William Hazlitt's essays; to have teetered on that same brink but to have written Gerard Manley Hopkins's poems—to live so close to nothing but to resist the urge to protect your gifts, keep them safe, wrap them in napkins—to have lived in such proximity to nothing, yet to have written a something, even a mini-something, but especially the glorious somethings of Hazlitt and Hopkins—maybe that is what it means, other disappointments notwithstanding, to enter into joy.*

Memory

I've got half a Hillshire Farm smoked sausage in the frying pan. My motivation is hunger and something like a metaphorical hunger for a memory of the taste. That would be enough, but as I was slicing the beef stick, I was returned to the first time I ever ate such a thing, at the local FoodTown, when I was, let's say, eleven years old. A young woman was offering free samples in a back corner of the store, somewhere near the open refrigerated sections with the cheeses, meats, and eggs, and my friend John Hickey and I were shamelessly eating as much as we could. I have never been able to recapture the exact magic of that moment, my first taste of the stuff. My smoked sausage slices always come out a little bit burned on the edges, a little too concaved from the cooking. But I try anyway, whenever I find it on sale. The woman that day was set up on a Formica table with spindly metal legs, with a small, square electric griddle coated in aluminum foil. In front of her, she set out the pieces of meat on a paper towel on a plate, with toothpicks stuck in them to keep things clean. I don't really remember all of this, or I can't be sure I do, but this is how the scene reconstitutes. What I remember most about that day, besides the delicious taste of the sausage slices, was what she said to John and me when we came back for our fourth or fifth slice: "You boys are eating up all of my profits." I can still recreate some semblance of the swing of her voice.

[Back in my kitchen, in my present, I have saved the sausages from the frying pan; now it is time to send them into my mouth! Into my head swishes the unfortunately memorable Roger Daltrey song "After the Fire," then my mind avoids the obvious detour to "Der Kommisar," sung by the *band* After the Fire, and is off to the recent Who reunion tour, which catapults me to their first of many farewell tours, in 1982, which I watched on HBO at John Hickey's house with my father's portable tape recorder propped in front of the tiny television speaker, recording the tinny ghost of what I thought would be a last chance.]

This was the first time I had heard that phrase, "eating up all my profits." I knew what profits were, but she was *giving* the sausage away. It seems strange to me that I should remember such an inanity, even more so because I didn't really understand what she meant. But the phrase stuck, stayed intact, verbatim, somewhere in my mind amidst the millions of other things people have said to me, sometimes people who mean a great deal to me, whom I love, yet whose sayings have gone utterly lost from my brain. How I would love to remember the first words my wife ever said to me, or her exact phrasing when she said yes, or my grandfather's last coherent sentences before he descended into darkness. Instead, I have "You boys are eating up all of my profits," from a young woman I never knew and could not recognize if I crossed her again.

Friedrich Nietzsche said, "Only that which never ceases to hurt stays in the memory." That sounds nice, has the right rhythm to reach for assertion and assurance, tastes pretty good on the tongue or in the brain, but, I'm sorry, Friedrich, what never ceases to hurt is what's gone.

Alfonsina y el Mar

Because of an odd series of coincidences, I am intimately familiar with the opening piano melody of Mercedes Sosa's "Alfonsina y el mar" ("Alfonsina and the sea") but I have never listened to the song all the way through. First of all, I used to have a phone with (relatively) little storage, so, even now that it has quadrupled, I have not yet downloaded any music. Nonetheless (and second of all), my wife, with whom I share so much, including six children and an iTunes account, has downloaded a number of songs, many of them from her childhood in Montevideo, and a few months ago she remembered Sosa's song, paid the ninety-nine cents, and added it to our cloud library. Next up (third), nearly every time I plug my phone into or connect its Bluetooth (signal?) to my car, it, or the car, supposes not that I want to listen to a podcast, as I have every single time before, but that I want my music, of which there is precious little; in fact, I am not even sure if my few Karina-purchased songs are resident on my phone or simply called down from the ether for live streaming. Finally (fourth), my uncustomized and largely ignored music library chooses always to order songs alphabetically, and while if this were really my music library it would find Galactic Cowboys' "About Mrs. Leslie," it instead finds Mercedes Sosa's lilting melody, a piano prelude that sets such a melancholic scene that I imagine a sad end for Alfonsina, and thus, today, as I write this essay, I should very much like to explore the song and see if I am right. Give me a few minutes . . .

It occurs to me that this essay (like all essays, if we generalize) will speak differently to readers familiar with Sosa and her song than it speaks to the ignorant, which I mean in the Spanish sense, which is passive and blameless, something you are, not something you can do, and which reminds us all that we are vastly ignorant, mostly through no fault of our own, and yet. It's what you do with/from/out of your ignorance that matters, by which I might mean learning or I might just as likely mean shut up and listen, and those may be the same thing. Either way, I aim (in my living and parenting and teaching and writing) for humility, which quality I have had to cultivate, insofar as it exists at all in me, which it certainly does, as it does in everyone, but perhaps not very much. I cannot be an impartial judge. In a world where even Mercedes Sosa, one of Argentina's best-known and most-beloved singers, came to me late and only coincidentally (and to you, perhaps, at one more level of remove, perhaps only right now), we must remind ourselves how small we are, which phrase I borrow from "Nightingale Song" by Toad the Wet Sprocket, which may be the most inane band name ever, as it was intended to be when Eric Idle wrote it as part of a "Rock Notes" sketch in *The Rutland Dirty Weekend Book* and, later, performed it on Monty Python's *Contractual Obligation Album*. He later said that he wanted "a name that would be so silly nobody would ever use it or dream it could ever be used. . . . And a few years later I was driving . . . in LA, and a song came on the radio, and the DJ said, 'That was by Toad the Wet Sprocket,' and I nearly drove off the freeway."

As it happens, Toad the Wet Sprocket, one of my favorite bands, made many significant songs, their lyrics often belying the frivolity of their name (or vice versa?), and if I'm honest, I must admit that singer Glen Phillips's melancholic vision of love and kindness and the noble impossibility of human understanding have deeply influenced me, sometimes in how they resonate with the ways I have felt, and sometimes in how they've taught me to see perspectives beyond my own. There is "Pray Your Gods," with its haunting rondo "*dona nobis pacem*" (put, in context, to far different use than in the canon), but before that, "i feel my body weakened by the years / as people turn to gods of cruel design / is it that they fear the pain of death / or could it be they fear the joy of life." There's a reminder to appreciate the simple things: "flowers in the garden / laughter in the hall / children in the park / i will not take these things for granted." There's religious questioning (about Paul) or spiritual perspective (about suffering) or righteous anger (about violence against women, or Leonard Peltier's imprisonment). There's even nostalgia for the present moment, in the example of "Walk on the Ocean" ("it seemed we'd already forgotten we came"), which I've evoked here mostly for its transitional properties, to get from "ocean" back to "Alfonsina and the sea," which by now I've listened to repeatedly as well as researched a bit. Perhaps you have, too.

How could I not have put it all together? I had all the ingredients, though distant, disorganized. Alfonsina is Alfonsina Storni. Have you heard of her? I have, though a bit vaguely. I've read some of her poems, both in classes and on my own, and I recall a general feeling of appreciation for their art and sentiment, though none of them sticks with me. Also I knew the legend of her death: that she walked calmly into the sea, or at least that's how her suicide had been portrayed, a kind of romanticized act of will in the face of terminal illness. As with all legends, this notion is only partly true.

Though biographers say that she jumped from a jetty, the popular account seems to have originated with Sosa's song, which was written by Ariel Ramírez and Félix Luna, and which posits vanishing footprints in the sand and "a path of sorrow and silence" leading to the depths. With its cast of sea snails and mermaids, the song wishes for, or perhaps creates, Storni's immortality, a calm and peaceful continuance, instead of a desperate end. The chorus, if it may be called that (the only verse sung twice), evokes a melancholy hope:

> Te vas Alfonsina con tu soledad,
> ¿qué poemas nuevos fuiste a buscar?
> Una voz antigua de viento y de sal
> te requiebra el alma y la está llevando
> y te vas hacia allá como en sueños,
> dormida, Alfonsina, vestida de mar.

Which is to say,

> Alfonsina, you're leaving with your solitude,
> What new poems are you searching for?

An ancient voice of wind and salt
Calls to your soul, carries it away,
And you follow as if dreaming,
Alfonsina, asleep, swathed in sea.

(This and other parts of the song allude to some of Storni's poems, most notably "Yo en el fondo del mar" ["Me at the bottom of the sea"] and her very last poem, "Voy a dormir" ["I am going to sleep"], which she mailed to *La Nación* in October 1938, shortly before her death, and which many see as a kind of suicide note.)

It seems that this essay has taken an unexpected turn, and I am now thinking about celebrity in a strange opposition to "real life," as we often take people whose talents we admire and whose work we consume to be of a different species, untouched by the events and emotions we ourselves feel. Who can know, but I suppose that Storni did not experience her death with anything like the poetic fancy (the calm resolution, the metaphorical vindication) ascribed to her in the song. Nevertheless, I also suppose I prefer the art of Sosa's singing to what my imagination conjures if I try to get all the way to any "real" Alfonsina in the moments before her death. And without the song and its serendipitous insistence every time I get in the car, I would not have understood, would not have made the connections to think upon this tragic figure. I believe I am the better for it.

To cut the sadness, I should like to share two brief experiences of interaction with two of the musicians I have mentioned above, whom I met and chatted with amiably, I believe, several times after their concerts, in my younger days, when such contact seemed, I don't know, more desirable or more permissible. I suppose I was simply enamored of their fame, in a cool way, but perhaps, too, I wanted to acknowledge their reality, approach them as a fellow human being.

But those meetings are not what I wish to relate. Years later, after Toad the Wet Sprocket had broken up and Glen Phillips had embarked on a solo career (about which only die-hard fans had any clue), I wrote him an email, commenting on the grammar of two yet-to-be-released songs of his (which I had heard in demo form, downloaded from his website). Who knows what possessed me to make such a mention? I hope it wasn't snark or superiority. But to his credit, Glen responded with humor and grace, lamenting that he'd recently committed the final, ungrammatical versions to tape (for release on an upcoming album), and adding

> P.S. If you want to get into some serious bad-writing territory, you might want to look into mixed metaphors. My personal low point is the song "Dam Would Break," a would-be emotionally moving song ruined by my mental sloth. The second verse reads: "What is this ice / that gathers 'round my heart / to stop the flood of warmth before it even starts / It would make me blind to what I thought would always be / the only constant in the world for me." Blindness has nothing to do with ice. I've taken to singing the word "numb" in place of "blind," but it shames me that the recorded and well distributed version of the song is so poorly written. There are numerous other metaphorical crimes in "Dam Would Break" and the majority of my other works, but in the words of one smarter than I: "I know it's only rock and roll, but I like it."

Phillips's realization looks a lot like the kind of comment I make a lot on essays I critique. "Corral your metaphors," I say. "Give them some relation to your subject, or at least a relation to one another." I invoke Alice Meynell's wisdom:

> Musicians know the value of chords; painters know the value of colors; writers are often so blind to the value of words that they are content with a bare expression of their thoughts, disdaining the "labor of the file," and confident that the phrase first seized is for them the phrase of inspiration.

Don't disdain the labor of the file, I say. Don't be too confident in the phrase first seized!

Nor in the path you'd envisioned for your essay. So I shall simply turn from the fading footprints on the beach to continue thinking about rock and rollers' lyrical choices. That long-ago mentioned song

"About Mrs. Leslie," by Galactic Cowboys, a band I loved when I was younger (and might love still if they were still around). Anyway. "About Mrs. Leslie": does the title sound familiar to you? If so, you probably recognize the 1954 movie of the same name. I've never seen it. Neither, I found out, has Ben Huggins, the band's singer, who accepts Facebook friend requests willy-nilly and who responded to my question with:

> At the time of the writing, Alan [Doss, the band's drummer] had only read the name of the movie in a TV Guide. So I made up a story about a boring old lady who sat around and drank tea with her friends. Then same suggested that we give her a dark little secret. Voila! A completely made up story about an old British lady with a dark secret.

. . . about whom we know nothing more than what the song suggests (she seems to be keeping her husband prisoner in a belfry, in a kind of simple twist on *Jane Eyre*, perhaps). Given that the song is only superficially inspired by the movie's title, it would be fruitless to seek intentional connections there. Perhaps, though, I might note the resonances between this appropriation and Ramirez and Luna's fanciful rendering of Alfonsina's last act: art is not life, even when drawn from life, or inspired by fragments of an external reality, but it diverges purposefully and is transformed, perhaps even transforms the material from whence it derives, so that hearers or readers, quite innocently, may eventually come to conflate the one with the other, or create connections unintended and invisible to the creators, or the livers. Perhaps there is something here about the inscrutability of representations, or presentations, such as one finds, to varying degrees, in characters both fictional and non-. Something about the need to make the attempt anyway, despite the impossibility of complete understanding. Something about the elusive, illusive variable effects of songs, which both reduce and expand, can only suggest, and yet convey quite a bit of . . . what? . . . emotion?

But an essay is not a song, so in the very least, I hold myself to the expectation that I not fabricate beyond the facts, as best I can ascertain them (an interesting word, *ascertain*, "to make certain," a concept antagonistic to good essayistic meandering), and I try not to make certain but to make sense. Somewhat.

> No me gustan las canciones porque mienten
> Porque todo se resuelve en tres minutos

> I don't like songs because they lie
> Because everything's resolved in three minutes
> —ANDRES CALAMARO, "Mi rock perdido"

What can we really know about anyone? What damage do we do when we presume to, when we "calculate others from ourselves" and find too late or too seldom that we've calculated wrong? How, then, is the world we perceive a distorted reproduction of ourselves? How is an act such as this, the writing of an essay, both futile and essential?

And this: if a five-second snippet of song can send the mind reeling on a twenty-five-hundred-word wondering where everything seems related and yet nothing seems resolved, perhaps we arrive only at Chesterton, recognizing/describing/excusing/asserting the essay that

> does not know what it is trying to find; and therefore does not find it.

Mea Culpa

As the phone calls, the letters, the legal summonses mount, and the Smoking Gun "journalists" harass me, my family members, and my friends, I have decided to come clean, to declare my guilt preemptively, before I am unmasked by those muckrakers with nothing better to do than to flush a fledgling writer's career down the toilet. I admit it: I fictionalized key parts of my supposedly nonfiction collection of personal essays, *Quotidiana.* As a longtime committed nonfictionist, one who teaches his students not to lie, to select and shape their real experiences into literature, I feel so ashamed. I sincerely apologize to those readers who have been disappointed in my actions.

What's perhaps most disappointing, to me at least, is that it's been my wife, my father, my mother-in-law, and a good friend who've tattled on me. For instance, on page 31, I claim that I only bought UB40's *Greatest Hits* when Karina and I were filling out our order of free CDs from Columbia House. Karina now assures me that, no, I actually bought this CD from a brick-and-mortar store as a gift for her. And on page 22, where I say that Karina gave our first son the nickname "Pato," I know now that I should have credited Karina's mother instead. I can only imagine the anguish I have caused unsuspecting readers who have taken my word for these events. Later in the book, on page 101, I write, perhaps erroneously, that "Helen sang alto harmony to my grandmother's soprano melody." Who knows why my father, who had read this particular essay in an earlier form, waited until the book was published to express his doubt about the veracity of this statement? Maybe, he told me, it was Helen who sang the soprano part. Or maybe not. The truth is, right now, we don't really know. Perhaps the Smoking Gun "investigators" can tell me for sure. And on page 65, at the end of a long, italicized list of Spanish names for fruits and vegetables for sale at Montevideo's Mercado Modelo, a section of the book that nobody actually reads, I briefly mention the Uruguayans' preferred word for pineapple, *ananá*, which I note in contrast to the more widely used *piña*. Although I have made no claim about the word's origin, my friend Eduardo Galeano, a wonderful Uruguayan writer, has nevertheless offered the following critique of my research:

> I like the book, but here's just a small observation: if I'm not mistaken, the word *ananá* is Guaraní, Tupí-Guaraní to be exact, because the fruit comes from Brazil and was unknown outside of tropical America before the European conquest.

I offer the correction or expansion here, in the spirit of penance for my sin of omission. But I suspect there is no forgiveness for the greatest factual error I've yet encountered in the book. On page 126, just joking around, I quote some lyrics from a Rush song, replacing "it's a part of us" with "hippopotamus." I attribute these lyrics correctly to Neil Peart, but place them in the song "Entre Nous," which is blatantly false and an embarrassment to me. I claim to be a staunch Rush fan, so how could I not know that these words are from "Different Strings," the song *after* "Entre Nous" on 1980's groundbreaking *Permanent Waves*? To this humiliating question I have no sufficient answer, only excruciating guilt and sorrow.

I regret my decisions to falsify my experience in these (and perhaps other, yet-undiscovered) ways, or my slothfulness in neglecting to check these vital facts of my life. I recognize that I have discredited myself in irreparable ways. I only hope these revelations will not alter my readers' faith in the book's central message, whatever that may be.

Thankfully, my publisher has assured me that it will take all steps necessary to put things right with the defrauded public. Taking a page from the Doubleday playbook, it's issued the following statement:

> The potential for controversy over Patrick Madden's *Quotidiana* will possibly in the future cause serious or perhaps only mild concern at the University of Nebraska Press. It is not the policy neither is it the stance of this or any other company that

we might or might not know of that it doesn't matter whether a book sold or lent from libraries as nonfiction isn't false, or that it might not be misconstrued as having arisen from certain unverities or misfacts. Readers wishing to receive a refund on their purchase should simply cut out the kookaburra from the book's jacket, paste it on a popsicle stick, and create a YouTube video of the animated bird chanting a page from *Quotidiana*, making sure to change voices for and properly cite any block-quoted passages. Send your link to refund@quotidiana.org along with your contact information. The best rendition (as voted on by a panel of expert judges) will receive a check for one-tenth of the book's current lowest Amazon Marketplace price. We try to bear a certain responsibility for some of what we publish, when we can, and we apologize to the reading public for any unintentional confusion, bewilderment, or mystification surrounding or concerning the publication of *Quotidiana* or any other books, ever.

Expectations (feat. Desirae Matherly)

My daughter loves this riddle I told her:

> You are driving a bus. At the first stop, 7 people get on. At the
> next stop, 3 more get on. At the third, 2 get off and 5 get on. At
> the fourth, no one gets on and 2 get off. At the fifth, 7 get off and
> 1 gets on. At the sixth stop, 2 get on and 2 get off. At the seventh,
> 10 people get on and 3 get off. What is the bus driver's name?

Reading it here, you can easily figure it out, because you can return
to the text and reread, but aloud, this gets people (nearly) every time,
because once they hear the numbers, they start trying to do arithme-
tic, thinking you're going to ask them how many people are left on
the bus. I apologize for stating the obvious. The point of the riddle
is misdirection, a subversion of expectations that's satisfying in its
cleverness instead of frustrating. This is just one example of this principle in action. One might easily point to most Hollywood movies,
for instance, with their twists and turns to keep viewers guessing. I
know this, and you know this, but I hope it's worth revisiting briefly
here, as I retread some of my own path to realizing it (making it real),
and applying it to essay writing, specifically.

Over the years, as I read and wrote and taught and critiqued
thousands of essays, I formulated an observation into a theory. For
context, you should know that, including graduate school, I've been
at this essay thing semiprofessionally for twenty years. Through
reading and writing countless good and bad examples, I came to feel
that the best essay endings worked their way backwards through the
text to shift a reader's understanding of the whole, to reconfigure
interpretation from a new insight. Thus, the endings were a surprise
that made sense; they granted an insight beyond what I would have
come to on my own, but not beyond what was reasonable. I became

fond of saying that this represented a surprising inevitability (or inevitable surprise).

While I never thought myself original for noticing this (and creating a handily chiasmic catchphrase to describe it), it took me quite a while to discover that Aristotle had theorized essentially the same thing in the *Poetics*:

> Such an effect [tragedy inspiring fear or pity] is best produced when the events come on us by surprise; and the effect is heightened when, at the same time, they follow as cause and effect. The tragic wonder will then be greater than if they happened of themselves or by accident; for even coincidences are most striking when they have an air of design. . . .
>
> A Complex action is one in which the change is accompanied by such Reversal, or by Recognition, or by both. These last should arise from the internal structure of the plot, so that what follows should be the necessary or probable result of the preceding action. It makes all the difference whether any given event is a case of propter hoc or post hoc.

That is, "because of this" versus simply "after this." We want causation, not simply correlation. "The king died and then the queen died" is not a proper story. No, wait. It *is* a story, according to Forster, but it's not a plot. A plot requires not only "a narrative of events arranged in their time-sequence," but a sense of causality ("then the queen died of grief"). For context, you should know that Aristotle's source texts were epic poems and plays, and Forster's focus was the novel, primarily. And here we are talking of essays, mostly, though the principles, as I have said, apply broadly.

Expectations affect not only endings, influence not only twists of plot and action. When we read, we bring myriad expectations to the text, from the most basic (that it will be decipherable), through the conventional (that it will exemplify proper grammar), through the contextual (that it will present to us a world we recognize or, sometimes, characters that we "relate to"), to the transcendental (that it will satisfy in us a spiritual yearning we didn't quite know we had). We read through our expectations at every turn, and every straightaway, too.

Still, we lose the thread sometimes, both in life and in art, when what we expect is continuity and we find the reverse; when a simple reunion with an old friend* brings the unexpected "I didn't know, I'm so sorry." Even though we might be the kind of people who listen to dreams, who buy new, larger cars when we get the feeling that we are headed for an accident, we fail to know about a friend's deep loss. (No one gets a pass.) "Had we been in our old car the child might have been—" The false assurance that sometimes what we intuit can lead us away from peril, weighed against the truth that we never know what to expect. The thief in the night is sometimes not a metaphor, it isn't the punch line of a joke but instead the grim march of if-onlys; it isn't a story about averting disaster but about taking it in the gut.

No one's expectations are infallible; no reader is ideal. Yet I am paid to read others' work and offer my honest critique, asking them questions and suggesting ways to improve. Perhaps the commonest category of misstep I find in draft work has to do with failing to meet or anticipate readers' expectations, failing to consider the expansiveness of language and the way ambiguities can be detrimental, even antagonistic to readers. I tell my students that I am a lazy, impatient, intentional misreader. I expect them to do the work of considering their words and phrases and rooting out unintentional misreadings. Because I will misread them every chance they give me, I say. We laugh, but they know I'm serious.

I find such problems all the time, but I suppose I ought to include here an example. So I've asked permission of one of my students, whose recent essay caused me and her classmates a slight bit of consternated amusement. The essay was titled "Love Bursts," which pressed PLAY on my mental boom box with a two-song playlist of Def Leppard's "Love Bites" and Nazareth's "Love Hurts," each of which strings together a litany of bad things love does (scars, wounds, marks, bleeds, brings me to my knees, etc.). (I could, too, have remembered the Everly Brothers' original "Love Hurts," or covers by Roy Orbison or Cher or . . . and who can forget the J. Geils Band's "Love Stinks"? [RIP J. Geils, who died only recently, and who was raised, I've just learned, in the next town over from my hometown in New Jersey.])

Anyway. "Love Bursts" seemed obviously a sentence, subject-verb. Bursting was something love did. This determined my reading. And the first section did nothing to revise my expectation, as the author returned to her childhood, to a night she spent with her aunt and cousins in a hotel. Her mother had allowed her to go only on the condition that she not wet the bed. Uh oh. You know what's going to happen next, don't you? Our narrative expectations are primed. But they're also confirmed in their reading of the title. Love *bursts* . . . we've got a bladder ready to *burst* in the nighttime, so . . . It's obvious.

Only it wasn't. The section ends in a display of auntly love, with smiles and bubble bath and not a hint of anger or frustration. Only later in the essay, two-thirds of the way through, does the title reconfigure into an adjective-noun phrase. It's been about bursts of love all along, but I didn't know it. I felt a bit misled. The author, knowing from the get-go how to apprehend the titular phrase, was surprised at my (and most of the class's) misreading. It's important to note that I don't believe her to be *wrong* with her title choice; I just want her to think more broadly about potential meanings.

The advice part of this essay will be brief and general ("feeling myself too ill-instructed to instruct others"—Montaigne): Try to be aware of the various readings and meanings readers may come to given your text. Understand language not as denotative but as accumulative and tentative, words in order forming constellations from which meaning emerges. Anticipate your readers' questions and objections, and avoid problems or address them as you write (perhaps even in direct address; the essay is wonderfully open to such metatextuality).

To wrap up, then: I love this story my mother told us kids. For context, you should know that for many years she worked as a secretary at a law firm that handled lots of motor vehicle cases.

You *need* to have uninsured motorist insurance. With the cases I see every day . . . there's a lot of people out there driving around without insurance, or without enough insurance. And if one of them hits you . . . you'll be on the hook for the damages. For years I kept telling Chris Leone, "Chris, you need to get uninsured motorist insurance," and she wouldn't listen. "Liz," she'd say. "You worry too much." But I kept telling her, for years, and finally she got uninsured motorist insurance.

You know what's going to happen next, don't you? And while you're sad for Chris, at least you're glad that she got uninsured motorist insurance just in time.

Except . . . in time for what? Nothing happened. Nobody hit Chris. Chris didn't hit anybody. "Mom!" we laughed. "This is the part where an uninsured motorist hits Chris's car, and . . ."

"No," said Mom. "That's it. She got the insurance. Now she's covered."

For context, you should know that recently my mother died of cancer. Because she had smoked almost her entire adult life, we long knew that the day would come, yet I echo what many have said: you're never really prepared. Despite the disarming pain that still catches me unawares and plunges me into a deep melancholy, I am grateful that her whole family—our father, and all of their children and our spouses, and their grandchildren, and many of her friends—gathered from near and very far to spend her last days with her, when she was still awake and aware and laughing and praying and telling us all how much she loved us. When she was gone, or nearly gone, I don't quite remember, we told this story to each other and it was a salve to our wounds.

I was so moved by this essay because I recall the birthday celebration for David in DC when I first learned that your mother had passed. I never expected that such an important loss would manifest in your life so early. I don't know why I thought you would be immune, but I remember feeling that I should have known, should have anticipated something. It's an irrational and empathetic response to the stupid, tragic fact of being alive and being human. I have often thought back to that night when I learned about your mother's death and felt that guilt† return. I'm still so sorry, so long after the news.

† I, too, feel a kind of guilt, because I hadn't told you sooner, or hadn't told you at all, really. I relied on the passivity of a Facebook post (ironic, perhaps, that at that time you had quit Facebook, when you were the friend whose recommendation convinced me to sign up years before), hoping, I suppose, to avoid the discomfort of telling friends, of putting them into that awkward position of not knowing what to say. But really, I think I have always fled from death, in ways that I am ashamed of but unable to overcome.

Freewill (feat. Joe Oestreich)

In memoriam: Neil Peart (1952–2020)

Somewhere, perhaps stashed away in an attic box, perhaps kicked under a car's front seat, perhaps decaying deep in a landfill, there's a cassette tape of Rush's *Permanent Waves* album that once belonged to my erstwhile friend Mike L. Young, who one afternoon escaped with me from a screening of *A Clockwork Orange* at Peter David's house, accidentally put his car in reverse instead of drive, and thus crashed into Pete's mother's car, causing dents and neck pain and a good bit of apologizing. I was sitting in the passenger seat when it happened, and because Mike's car radio didn't work, I had just pressed PLAY on the boom box he kept there for musical accompaniment. That day's somewhat arbitrary choice was "Freewill." With the crash, I quickly decided to stop the music, but my finger slipped slightly, pressing RECORD on top of the already depressed PLAY, and because Mike was not a huge Rush fan, had not actually bought the album himself but had recorded it on a blank tape, we were left with a perfectly timed set of new lyrics inserted into the descending scale outro:

> Da-na-na-na-na-na-na-na
> Da-na-na-na-na-na-na-na
> Mike: "My mirror fell off!"
> Me: "Wait"
> Dunhhhnhhhnhhh

Is *erstwhile* an appropriate word to convey a friendship lost but never broken? Mike was a year ahead of me in high school, and I was absent, living in Louisiana, during my freshman and sophomore years, and we lived in neighboring New Jersey towns, so we overlapped only between fall 1987 and summer 1988, during which time we were on the track team together. We were both tall and a bit uncoordinated, fairly good at school, perhaps *geeky* is an accurate catchall adjective.

We got along well, if not spectacularly, and once he graduated, I saw him rarely and eventually never again.

While we're here, let us take an associative jaunt together, reader, understanding that there is no whole to be comprehended, no essential destination, and that what you read is only a shadow and approximation, a selection and translation of the memories I have here revived or the thoughts currently and recently swirling around my head, so that it is no detour to think linguistically instead of narratively. It is the inevitable path of the essay.

I never think of the word *erstwhile* without it bringing along its cousin *ersatz*, and vice versa, so that I always have to look them up, to be sure of myself, or, barring that, sure of their definitions. They really shouldn't be too difficult to remember, given the *-while* in *erstwhile*, which should indicate time, as in "once upon a time," or even the *erst*, which suggests (and indeed shares a root with) *ere* and *early* and, more strictly, *earliest*. *Ersatz*, you might suspect from its spelling, comes from a somewhat different history, via the German, meaning "replaced" or "re-seated," though its *er* derives, too, from *early*, so that we get (from only a century ago) its current meaning of "replacement or substitute (usually of an inferior quality)."

And either or both of those words always shuffle my mind linguistically to remember my college English professor Erskine Peters, whom I didn't know well, but who was pleasant and excited about even a survey of American literature, and who introduced me to both canonical and noncanonical, particularly African American, literature, in a time when I was a physics major and avid reader, but barely had a notion of the great works. I recall only one conversation I had with him, during which I asked if he knew of his inverted namesake, Peter Erskine, a jazz drummer whom I'd never heard but had read about in one of the drumming magazines I'd picked up because it featured Rush's Neil Peart on the cover. He *had* heard of him, he said. And that, as I recall, was that. I had nothing to add and neither did he.

I have learned in the course of writing this essay that Dr. Peters died just five years after I knew him, of pneumonia, at the age of forty-nine, or exactly my age when this essay will be published, assuming I make it. I feel a touch of sadness, of course, but also a recognition that the only thing that has changed is my knowledge. He's been gone for over twenty years, and though I've thought of him from time to time, I have never made an attempt to reach out or find him until now. In a sense, to me he's remained real and in this world. Now, as I approach him not as an ignorant student but as an initiated peer in academia, I find that among his four books (I had neither considered nor cared that my professors might be authors in their own right), there is the brief *Fundamentals of Essay Writing: An Orientation Manual*, which seems intended to convince reluctant high schoolers that writing is important and potentially rewarding. I think I would have liked to sit down with my former teacher to discuss such essayistic things. He would not remember me, of course, but he might be tickled that, like him, I've made a life from literature. Perhaps he would be ever so slightly pleased that we have visited him here in this essay.

I have also learned that in his lifetime, Neil Peart has had three drum teachers. The first, Don George, he studied with beginning at age thirteen. Then for thirty years he taught himself by listening to drummers he admired and subverting and complicating expectations for the Rush songs he played on. His drumming, always intricate and powerful, was respected by fans and fellow musicians alike, earning him numerous "best drummer" awards and a spot in the *Modern Drummer* hall of fame. But after "bluffing" [his word] his way through a Buddy Rich tribute concert and album, he decided to sign up for lessons from Freddy Gruber, a contemporary of Buddy Rich and, like him, a former big band jazz drummer. As this went well ("I completely rebuilt my drumming from the ground up. I feel like I've started over as a beginner."), a decade later he sought another teacher. He chose another Gruber pupil, whom we've mentioned just above, jazz drummer extraordinaire Peter Erskine. Of his first three-hour lesson, he mentions only learning to keep quarter-note time on a ride cymbal without waving his wrist. He was sent home with homework, which he was to do only on a high-hat, so that's all he played for two months: high-hat exercises. No drums. No other cymbals. Just high-hat. When he returned for his next lesson, he'd made significant progress, enough to earn a "perfect" judgment from Erskine. More homework, more high-hat practice, and he found himself back at Erskine's studio for a third lesson, during which he got to play a full drum set to accompany "Love for Sale." He knew the song, had played it plenty, but only on high-hat. I was not there, so I cannot really comment, but Peart claims that his performance was a struggle. Next, Erskine sat at the kit and played it himself. "His playing was delicate, eloquent, and economical," Peart reports, "a kind of artful, effortless surgery that expressed supreme musicality."

Do you distract yourself from important tasks with YouTube videos like I sometimes do? I ask because if you're going to do that anyway, you might as well look up some Peter Erskine videos like I've been doing. Because I'm no drummer, I can barely begin to understand the magic of his playing, but I can also report that he manages to woo me, to entrance me, with his, yes, "effortless" style. He seems to be an embodiment of rhythm. The sticks and drums are not external to him, not appendages. Drummer and drums are unified, one and the same.

Of course, Peart's no slouch at all, and the fact that he chose to humble himself, surrender his renown and subject himself to teachers later in life, speaks well of him.

Where was I going with all this? I'm not quite sure. Perhaps it's sufficient (he says after a three-page linguistic detour sparked by his *own* choice of the word *erstwhile*!) that we've explored connections, learned a thing or two, found some metaphors to keep in the bank for possible future use.

But let's get back to that song, "Freewill," something of a rarity in rock music, in that its lyrics are (ersatz?) philosophical, not carnal. This quality, along with its musical surprises and subversions, is what appealed and continues to appeal to me. Its message stems from lyricist and drummer Peart's disaffection from religion, in part, and his assertion of independent thinking. For a teenager like me, eager to find direction and confirmation of my value, the song was an inspiration on all fronts and a "ready guide" on this "fortune hunt that's far too fleet." With this and so many other Rush songs, I made myself apprentice to Peart's teachings. But the record sleeve in the United States, at least for a time, printed the wrong words in the chorus. Instead of

If you choose not to decide you still have made a choice,

which is obviously what Geddy Lee sings, the liner notes say

If you choose not to decide you cannot have made a choice

an unfortunate typo that effectively reverses the meaning. I recall reading a Rush Backstage Club newsletter in which a fan asks for clarification on the discrepancy, and Peart, whose album, I'd assume, came from Canada and had the correct lyrics, doesn't understand the question. He takes it to be a mishearing rather than a misprinting, and thus responds that "other than perhaps dropping an 'and' or a 'but,' we take great care to make the lyric sheets accurate."

I mention this little mishap because this phrase became the source of a friendly online debate recently, when my writing colleague Joe Oestreich posted near election time that

> Re: Voting. My man Neil Peart once wrote, "If you choose not to decide, you still have made a choice." My man Neil Peart is full of shite.

I didn't know Joe very well, but because of my deep love of Rush and my honest confusion at Joe's meaning, I posted a follow-up asking for clarification. Joe humbly obliged, and it soon became clear that he and I had differing, nearly opposite, interpretations of that line. What's more, it had never occurred to me that there could even *be* another interpretation, and it's probably safe to say that Joe felt the same way.

We're talking nuance here, but let me try to explain what took us several back-and-forths to figure out. When I hear that line, I imagine it as a kind of reprimand, or a takedown. *You might think you can get away without choosing, but you can't. Even not choosing is a choice.* In the context of a song about free will, this seems to work. What's more, I hear it as antagonistic. If you're the kind of person who wants not to choose, you're not Neil Peart's friend. It's a bad idea to try to escape choice. And if you stubbornly refuse (perhaps in Joe's context, of voting), then you choose the status quo. Thus you should make an active choice (cast your ballot or determine your worldview or accept responsibility for your actions). This is what I've always understood from that line.

Joe understood it differently. I'll let him explain:

Back [when I was a teenager] I assumed that "If you choose not to decide, you still have made a choice" meant that not choosing (which is an "act" that seems passive on the surface) is actually an active stance, which is to say not choosing is making a choice about:

1. the nature of choice in and of itself and
2. the merit of the available options one is being asked to choose among (i.e. choosing not to decide is a de facto acknowledgement that all options are bad, or, at minimum, worse than abstaining).

So, back then I thought Peart meant that not choosing to decide was okay and maybe even admirable. When I posted my Facebook update, saying that Neil was full of shite, that's what I meant: He's full of shite if his lyric means that not choosing is an acceptable choice when it comes to voting.

Because when it comes to the ballot, choosing not to decide is a chickenshit stance. The fact is, in an election, a decision is going to be made whether you participate or not, so forgoing what little power you have by choosing not to decide is not okay. It's not admirable. It's not a valid choice. Even if all options are some degree of bad, you owe it to society to actively choose the least bad option. Or else you and everyone else might get stuck—partially because of the voters who refused to weigh in—with the worst option. I was thinking specifically of people who disliked both Hillary and Trump and therefore stayed home, choosing not to decide between the two, which, of course, left us with Trump.

I can see this point, too, now, though it had never occurred to me before. Which I find fascinating. That for thirty-odd years, Joe and I read these lyrics in different ways, each available and justifiable given the text itself, but neither of us was aware of the ambiguity that might lead to the other's interpretation. And while in a way, Joe has come around to my view on the line, I don't really think this is a matter of right and wrong, even if Peart himself, if he were asked, might assert one meaning over the other. In a way, I am choosing now to allow variant, even mutually exclusive, meanings to occupy my mind simultaneously, partly because I think I might find them useful in different contexts, and partly because I'm on a lifelong quest to live up to John Keats's ideal, to be "capable of being in uncertainties, mysteries, doubts, without any irritable reaching after fact and reason."

So anyway, that's a choice I'm making, not in a particular moment, not in response to confrontation, but in general and long-term. Perhaps if pressed, I might resolve the uncertainty a particular way for a particular purpose (just as I might head to the polls or mail in my ballot), but the resolution would be temporary, which, it occurs to me now, might, Schrödinger-like, describe all resolutions. After all, during the vast majority of our time, we attend only to a very few things while all others fade to the background, which might be effectively nonexistence. While I can posit intellectually that Mike L. Young's Rush cassette still exists somewhere in the world, even if it has decayed or altered its form, I can also ask: does it *really*? If a tree falls in the forest . . . And if a cassette molders in a landfill with no one to press PLAY, does it make a sound?

In Step with ... Montaigne
(feat. David Lazar)

On a pleasant afternoon outside Bordeaux, in his tower at the corner of his family chateau, the writer and statesman Michel de Montaigne, stocky and bedraggled in britches and poofy blouse, was serving us wine from the estate's northerly vineyards.

"I speak my mind freely on all things, even those which perhaps exceed my capacity and which I by no means hold to be within my jurisdiction," he assured us as he wandered to a shelf and began fidgeting with a book of Cicero's poems. "I set forth notions that are human and my own, simply as human notions considered in themselves, not as determined and decreed by heavenly ordinance ... as children set forth their essays to be instructed, not to instruct."

The beloved former mayor and adviser to French kings is perhaps best known for his three-volume collection of *Essays*, which he began writing upon his retirement in 1572, at the age of thirty-seven, when he discovered that simply allowing himself idle time to read and think led his mind, "like a runaway horse, [to] give itself a hundred times more trouble than it took for others, and [to] give birth to so many chimeras and fantastic monsters, one after another, without order or purpose," that he began to write in order to "make [his] mind ashamed of itself."

His first two volumes of *Essays*, which appeared in 1580, contained this prefatory warning: "Reader, I am myself the matter of my book; you would be unreasonable to spend your leisure on so frivolous and vain a subject." Yet readers did spend their leisure on reading the *Essays*, enjoying Montaigne's candor; his wavering even-handedness;

his playful, associative mind on display in the text. And not only in France in the sixteenth century, but around the world and through the centuries.

This simple man of letters seems as surprised as anyone that his literary legacy has lasted over four hundred years. "I do not love myself so indiscriminately, nor am I so attached and wedded to myself, that I cannot distinguish and consider myself apart, as I do a neighbor or a tree," he commented as he poured refills then tenderly passed us an original printing of his book. "Here you have some excrements of an aged mind," he chuckled, "now hard, now loose, and always undigested." And we all had a hearty laugh together.

Personal

Born February 28, 1533, in Guyenne, France. Married to Françoise de la Chassaigne (1565–92), with six children, one who survived infancy.

Why You Know Him

In his *Essays*, Michel performs acrobatic mental feats of association, considering everything that comes into his purview with artless art and graceless grace. "It is the language of conversation transferred to a book," said Emerson. "Cut these words, and they would bleed."

What You Don't Know

Out of respect for her honor, I have never gazed upon the breasts of Mme. De Montaigne.

I will not sit with thirteen at the table. I can dine without a tablecloth, but very uncomfortably without a clean napkin. My teeth . . . have always been exceedingly good. . . . Since boyhood I learned to rub them on my napkin, both on waking up and before and after meals. I am not excessively fond of either salads or fruits, except melons.

My meat: rare.

Favorite movies?

I was expecting more, or perhaps less, from *Stoic*. Perhaps the prison film is not my genre. *The Cannibals* was interesting in a lurid way, surprising in its Sophoclean inspiration. I frankly thought there would be more about the cannibals. Perhaps I'm too literal about these things. *A Man for All Seasons* was one I watched several times. It reminded me that as an ill conscience fills us with fear, so a good one gives us greater confidence and assurance.

When I dance, I dance, when I sleep, I sleep, and I think Fred Astaire is like a sleep dancer, walking on air . . . that magical man. He seems to stop time. So, I'd say *Swing Time* is a good one, with Ginger Rogers . . . I am very much driven by beauty. So let's just say anything with Rita Hayworth. The felicity that glitters in virtue, shines throughout all her avenues and ways. Oh, and "Put the Blame on Mame"!

What books are on your nightstand these days?

I study myself more than any other subject.

Understood, but any books grabbing you lately?

Erasmus, Rabelais, La Boetie . . .

What do you think of more contemporary essayists, say, James Baldwin?

If you press me to say why I loved him, I can say no more than because he was he, and I was I. I also quite like that fellow Sebald.

We understand that your tastes in music run from des Prez and Willaert to more contemporary fare. Can you share with us some of your favorite popular songs?

"Boys, Boys, Boys," by Lady Gaga would seem to capture the essence of the Socratic impulse. Then there's "I Just Don't Know What to Do with Myself," by the White Stripes. Lisa Hannigan's "I Don't Know" is quite good. Dusty Springfield sang a song very true to my way of thinking, "How Can I Be Sure." Then, of course, Ray Charles singing

"You Don't Know Me" speaks to me of the wavering and noncommittal natures we carry in this shifting world. Similarly, the Clash's "Should I Stay or Should I Go" comes from a dilemma I have often found myself contemplating.

So this recent book, *After Montaigne* . . . what do you think
of the use of your work as the basis for new musings?

I seek in books only to give myself pleasure by honest amusement. I seek only the learning that treats of the knowledge of myself. [*After Montaigne*] has this notable advantage for my humor, that the knowledge I seek is there treated in detached pieces that do not demand the obligation of long labor, of which I am incapable.

I find it admirable at representing to the life the movements of the soul and the state of our characters. I cannot read it so often as not to find in it some new beauty and grace.

Amongst so many borrowed things, I am glad if I can steal one, disguising and altering it for some new service. All the glory that I aspire to in my life is to have lived it tranquilly. There is nothing that poisons a man so much as flattery.

But I'm flattered.

Timing

The first goal on the 2014 Madden Family European Road Trip Vacation (after my semester directing a study abroad program in Madrid) was my pilgrimage to Montaigne's tower in the Perigord region east of Bordeaux. We arrived after a long day in the car and were surprised to find a chain blocking the entrance. Turns out the site was closed not just on Mondays, as David Lazar had warned me, but on Tuesdays as well. After a few minutes of pleading in fake French, I got to speak to the gardener, who spoke English, and who graciously led us on a tour of the grounds, including some wild- and tame-life encounters (birds, lizards, a snake, and several donkeys). I told him how I was a disciple of Montaigne, wrote my own essays, was editing a book paying homage to the master essayist. He said he wasn't much for reading Montaigne, but he sure liked caring for the plant life around his place. Laurent's patience and kindness were extraordinary, and as my family turned finally to leave, he gave me, a lifelong teetotaler, a bottle of Chateau Michel de Montaigne wine (2001 vintage). In all, it was an utterly pleasant afternoon, despite my getting so close but failing to visit the tower.

The way I figure, I can take this thwarted pilgrimage two ways. I can be disappointed, upset, what have you, or I can do like an essayist and use what really happened to my benefit. Like Alexander Smith said of Montaigne:

> Each event of his past life he considers a fact of nature; creditable or the reverse, there it is; sometimes to be speculated upon, not in the least to be regretted. If it is worth nothing else, it may be made the subject of an essay.

Or as Paul says (in my paraphrased appropriation):

All things work to the good of them that love the essay.

When I set out, I had hoped to see with my own eyes the inscriptions in the beams of Montaigne's library. Sure. But had I joined a regular tour, I'd never have met Laurent. I'd have been processed through the attraction like so many glassy-eyed high-school kids. I'd have paused and examined, yes, and I'd have taken some pictures, but I did those things anyway, from outside the walls, and one of the things I considered is this:

That there's something appropriate about being stymied in an essayistic quest, because essays were never about completing things; they distrust the very notion of tidy endings. Much better, it seems to me now, that I missed the dusty tower and instead strolled the grounds with the gardener, who, like the Great Dead Man he and I serve, contains within him the entire human condition.

Inertia

Without quite realizing it, over the past dozen years I've been training my body to automatically close my office door with the ideal amount of effort, imparting the exact momentum for the task. I should clarify. I swing the door shut as I'm leaving, aiming for the sweet spot, the gentle click, with nary a harsh slam and ne'er a miss, because, in this hurried age, who has time to pause and hold the handle all the way, or, worse, to return to finish the ajarring job? My timing had become impeccable. As I'd sling on my backpack and slide out the door, I'd reach back with my left hand, catch the handle, and, without breaking stride, flick slightly towards me. I'd not even turn back; I'd just hear the satisfying kiss of snug contact and know that I'd left my things locked safely inside.

Grammarians such as myself may have noticed the verb tense in the previous sentences, especially "had become," which says more than it denotes, I think. Why, we must ask, is the narrator's timing no longer impeccable? What trouble do these tenses portend?

[As an essay classicist, I often claim to be allergic to drama, suspense, all the trickery of a writer's sleight of hand, and yet I must realize, too, that such is inevitable, if only in its purely grammatical forms.]

> Most of the occasions for the troubles of the world are grammatical.
> —MONTAIGNE, "Apology for Raymond Sebond"

Speaking of Montaigne, it's his fault. That my door no longer closes all the way, that in the past weeks, I've repeatedly heard no click, had to stop, turn around, and thrust my hand back to the handle to close the door firmly and finally. I'd calculate that I've lost a good minute of quality time, all told.

It's Montaigne's fault, I realized (after several confused days discovering that, then wondering how, I'd lost the touch), because I've got a Montaigne costume hanging on the back of the door. For years it wasn't there, but now it's there, so I've added weight to the door, thereby increasing its moment of inertia.

"Moment of inertia" resonates with the title of this essay, so now I've partially resolved that little (perhaps unformed) question you may have been carrying since you started reading. The object of the detective's quest you unwittingly set out upon begins to clarify. At the very least, you know to pay attention to the phrase. Perhaps you recall, from physics class, that "moment of inertia" describes a body's resistance to angular acceleration. The "inertia" part echoes Newton's first law of motion: "An object at rest remains at rest, and an object in motion remains in motion, unless acted upon by an unbalanced force." More popularly, we think of *inertia* as immobility, stagnation, idleness, or at least resistance to motion. It is something to be overcome. The "moment" in the phrase refers to the product of a force acting at a distance from a reference point (to produce a rotational acceleration). As far as I can ascertain, it has nothing to do with the *moments* we're used to, the brief units of time, the ones that inexorably add up to our lives, that fly till they run out their race. And the phrase entire? "Moment of inertia"?

Certainly we can recognize a metaphor when it's staring us in the face?

Hold on a moment, though! Did you say Montaigne *costume?*

Yes, I did. That is the result of the lovely confluence of several felicitous happenstances.

Where to begin? Ah:

1. One day in the hallway I ran into Bob Hudson wearing an ornate French Renaissance outfit, accoutrement of his teaching that day. I expressed my admiration, and he explained its provenance: a student had asked to create the costume for her final class project. Bob bought the fabric. She got an A.

2. Soon after, I was asked to give the keynote address at the English department awards banquet. Itching (as always) to subvert expectations and bring a bit of humor to the typically humdrum, I enlisted the aid of my friend and colleague Joey Franklin, who, 3. with his close-cropped "thinning" hair, though without a goatee, looks remarkably like Michel de Montaigne. We borrowed Bob's blouse, bought a fake moustache, and convinced the theater department to lend us a ruff, then set him up in a nearby room on a laptop, poised to "interrupt" my dignified discourse with an "ill-timed" Skype call. So there I was, droning away to the assembled honorees on the importance of Montaigne, paging through PowerPoints projected behind me to the big screen, when there erupted a startling sound and appeared a pop-up window. Flustered, embarrassed, apologizing, I took the call, marveling at the serendipity. "How appropriate," I said to Montaigne (to the audience). "I was just telling these people about you!"

I wish you could have been there. The crowd was at first mortified, then confounded, then relieved once they realized the shtick. Holding attention with the spectacle, Montaigne and I conversed at length on topics of wide interest, such as the empathic influence of essays, the charms and perils of idleness and attentiveness, the need for balance, the interconnectedness of all things. Joey's French accent is peccable. Somewhere between Inspector Clouseau and Pepe le Pew.

4. After that successful trial run, I (re)discovered that Shelli Spotts, a graduate student in the BYU creative writing program, was (remains) a talented costume designer. I asked her if she'd be willing to make a Montaigne costume; she agreed, and 5. the English department let me use research funds to pay for it. Shelli modeled the garb on the famous 1580 portrait (copied several times later) featuring a rather dour Montaigne gussied up in his finery, including a satiny puffy overcoat, burgundy on its right sleeve and ivory on its left.

After (surprise) appearances at the NonfictioNOW Conference in Flagstaff, the AWP Conference in

Los Angeles, another keynote at our sister school (BYU–Idaho), plus a lead role in perhaps the silliest book trailer ever made [see https://youtu.be/K9ccJA3dQak], the costume now hangs in its dry-cleaner's bag on the back of my door, messing up my muscle memory.

I suppose I could store the clothes elsewhere, at home or in Joey's office, and perhaps I will, though I feel a fleeting glee every time I glance over my shoulder to my door and see the outfit hanging there, along-side portraits of my children and below a copy of the dot-matrix sign my father years ago hung in all his children's bedrooms admonishing DO IT NOW! *DO IT QUICKLY*, in response to our general lackadaisy, our tendency to ignore chores, refuse requests, or to get caught up in too many tasks, then complain about our lack of time. Little did we know, my father knew. I smile at the incongruities of existence, the recursions and extrapolations, the way experience seems to close upon itself but refuses to shut, remains open, confounds our automatic responses, demands our attention, the action of a thoughtful mind some distance from events. I think, also, to Montaigne's office, with

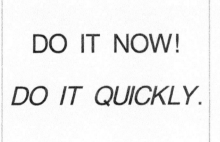

its inscriptions in the rafters, words to live and write by, such as I DO NOT UNDERSTAND; I PAUSE; I EXAMINE. Which humble habit, though it opposes my father's fine advice, fits the essaying process aptly, admirably, as well as enacts the metaphor we seemed to have abandoned paragraphs ago.

Seemed to, grammarians might note.

Thumbs (feat. Elena Passarello & Wendy S. Walters)

Thumb, for its similarity to *some,* provides a ready linguistic pun, when one makes the name change, when one is in a mood for thumb humor.

Perhaps the most difficult *thumb-*for*-some* switch would be the word *something,* rendered *thumbthing,* as in "Thumbthing in the way she moves / Attracts me like no other lover."

Sinatra, it is said, once sang it as a cover, claiming that it was his favorite Lennon/McCartney composition. Harrison, in his typical grace and humility, did not mind. He had a good laugh about it, thumbed his nose at the whole fame-and-ego trip. He was never one to stick out.

Me, I frankly prefer any number of Harrison songs. "Here Comes the Sun," for instance. "Taxman." "Think for Yourself." Of "Thumbthing," only the bridge appeals to me, and then only musically. "You're asking me will my love grow." The answer: "I don't know, I don't know."

Because she almost lost her thumb. How it happened was. She put her thumb out there, held it up to the window to make sure her sense of direction was still working. There might have been a song for it, but she didn't know her part. The bit of the thumb that matters most. From inside the house she would never know she was headed in the wrong direction. All sign posts turned against her. Beneath her flesh, the bone stood erect, this time by her choice. Of course, that was the song she should have known to sing, but she sang the other one—the song about taking. As if the grip made a difference. She trusted that any slip of the fist made her look stronger. Even when she was letting go. I mean, she heard the music in her head. I

*Good Night My
    Thumb-Bone.*

You Do Thumbthing to Me.

Thumbthin' Else.

*Thumbday My Prince
    Will Come.*

*Gimme Thumbthing
    to Believe In.*

*Wanna Be Startin'
    Thumbthing.*

*Thumbthing Tells Me I'm
    into Thumbthing Good.*

Under My Some.

*You Got Your Next Trick on
the Tip of Your Some.*

Ridin' Somes.

Suck on My Some.

Tub Something.

All Somes.

Just Like Tom Some's Blues.

*You can fool all of the people
thumb of the time, and
thumb of the people
all of the time, but you
can't fool all of the
people all of the time.*

*There's a place for us
thumbwhere.*

*Thumb people wait a lifetime
for a moment like this.*

*Everybody wants thumb;
I want thumb too.*

*Thumber breeze make
me feel fine.*

*Thumb people like to rock;
thumb people like to roll.*

*don't know, I don't know. It did not matter when she
was the only one. She had never been ready to work
like the rest. Here to serve, albeit in her own groove.
She hated to say she tried, why the sound kept slipping away.*

I wonder: Would we thumb our noses still if not for the
phrase? *Does* anybody really thumb their nose anymore?

Corollary to thumb humor is thumbprint art, a
malaise that flared up during my middle-school years
and which seems to have been eradicated in most first-
world countries. "Thumbody loves you," declared a pink
whorl with line-drawn arms and legs, cheeky smile,
perhaps a shock of hair. I think I can remember an early
understanding of the double meaning: thumb-body, a
body that's a thumb!

Quite a different connection comes to me today. I
notice there is only one b. I attach it to the *thum*, leaving thumb-ody. *Ody* can take me either to Garfield or
to Latin, by way of Spanish, where *odio* is hate. I come
back to English, where *odious* is hateful, and I have a
satisfactory judgment on the cutesy creatures.

There's another song that's been clamoring for my
literary attentions as the priest across the aisle from
me susurrs—*what?* the rosary?—as he fiddles with
his glasses, adjusts the airflow from above, thumbs
through his scriptures. "Don't you want thumbody to
love?" asked Jefferson Airplane, when they were still
legitimate, before they started name-changing.

It was a common question for the time. Speaking of
those questions without answers, what is with Ringo
stalling his mates. "Do you need anybody?" they ask in
three-part harmony. "I need thumbody to love." "Could
it be anybody?" "I just need thumbone to love." Or is
it thumb-bone?

Smells

BY MICHEL DE MONTAIGNE

translated by Stephen de Haynie & Patrick de Madden

ᴬ Alexander the Great had his PR guys spread the rumor that his sweat not only didn't stink, it smelled good, because his body was better than everyone else's. Plutarch and others tried to find the cause of that sweet sweat. But with most people, the best smell is no smell at all, as my father used to say. For instance, I know this woman whose halitosis strikes you from across the room, but she doesn't seem to notice, and nobody tells her, and she's always trying to talk right up in your face. I wish Plautus were still living, so he could subtly hint that maybe she should brush her teeth:

A woman smells best when she doesn't smell

Foul odors probably smell worse to the blind, because their other senses are heightened to make up for their lack of sight. And we shouldn't invest our money with those people who wear perfumes; they're trying to mask some defect in their natural state. If you don't believe me, just ask the ancient poets, who were always saying stuff like "To smell good is to stink" and

You think it's funny that we do not smell, Coracinus?
Well, I'd rather walk around unscented.
It's harder for the bloodhounds to track you that way.
MARTIAL

And now for something completely different:

If you think that smells good, Posthumus, you're going
to be sitting alone at home every Friday night.
MARTIAL

^B But I actually like sweet-smelling things, like those magic markers that smell like cherries, or oranges, or lavender, and I really hate bad smells, which is why it's so unfortunate that I usually catch a whiff of something foul before anyone else does.

> *Whoever smell't it dealt it.*
> HORACE

^C Simple, natural smells are best, especially with the ladies (Hey, ladies!). A friend of mine said that the Scythian women used to perfume their entire bodies with herbs, and I believe him, because he is very smart and does his own taxes. When these women approached men, even after bathing, they were sleek and sweet-smelling.

^B Whatever the odor, it's amazing how it sticks to me and how my skin drinks it in. All those protestors in the town square, camping out and playing those incessant drums, really should stop complaining that Nature has left us without any way to convey smells to our nose, because it's completely unnecessary. Smells can convey themselves just fine. And for crying out loud, have these hippies never noticed that their scraggly mustaches perform that function? If I touch my mustache with my gloves or handkerchief, the smell will remain all day, sitting there just under my nose, the worst place for it to be when it smells bad, although it would probably look strange anywhere else, such as on my cheek, although I suppose a unibrow is a kind of displaced mustache, still, it doesn't look good there, does it? I think there's a gas leak somewhere. When I was younger, all those delicious, greedy, and gluttonous kisses used to stick to the 'stache, reigniting passion with every inhalation. And yet, I am little subject to popular diseases, the ones that get invited to all the parties, the ones transferred by conversation or the air; I have been safe from those of my time, even though they've infected large populations in our armies and our city. ^C We read of Socrates that he never left Athens during the plague years, and yet he never got sick.

^B Doctors could probably get a lot more use out of odors than they do, and if not, then the multilevel marketers will take over. Medicines smell strong sometimes, and vapors can be used to clear the head.

Because these smells change me sometimes and uplift my spirits, I approve of lighting incense in churches in old religious nations and hippie communes (but, please, stop those useless protests against Nature already!), because they cleanse us and make us better for contemplation.

[c] I would have liked to eat with those chefs who season the meat they cook with such savory odors, as Roy of Thunes did at his BBQ last summer, to which I was not invited but heard about from a guy who undoubtedly isn't as partyworthy as I am. Roy cooks really nice smelling meats, like peacock and pheasants, and the rich odors spread throughout the castle and into the neighborhoods and linger there for hours.

[B] What I am saying is that I refuse to stay in a hotel that smells funky. I used to like Venice and Paris a lot more before I actually went there and realized how bad they smell. The first one smells of a marsh, and the other of mud. If I want to smell mud, I can just go into the woods and lie down next to the stream.

The Proverbial _____

If you can't beat a dead horse, join him

Never talk to a gift horse with food in its mouth

A bird in the hand is worth beating around the bush

A barking dog never bites off more than it can chew

Rhonda helps those who help themselves

It is easier for a camel to enter the kingdom of heaven than for a rich man to find a needle in a haystack

Build a better mousetrap and the world will beat a
path to hell, paved with good intentions

Out of sight, out of the mouths of babes

You can't have your heart out and eat it too

Don't count your chickens before they cross the road

Let the chip on your shoulder fall where it may

One bad apple doesn't fall far from the tree

Take time to smell the grindstone

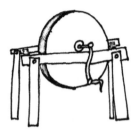

Laughter is a taste of your own medicine

A bat in the hand is worth two out of hell

You made your bed, now let sleeping dogs lie in it

Curiosity killed two cats with one stone

A rolling stone gathers no rosebuds while it may

A stitch in time is on my side

Don't bite off more than the hand can feed you

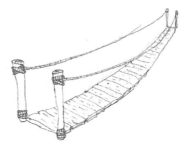

We'll burn that bridge when we come to it

Poetry

The other day as we left the doctor's office, my seven-year-old daughter, Adriana, brushed past me, pronouncing to the air: "I've never seen the top of my head." She kept on her way to the car, without pause, without a sidelong glance to find an answer or a response. I smiled and caught the essay she had given me.

I suspect that I *have* seen the top of my head, in a mirror or in a photograph, but I have no distinct memory of such a thing. Today, if I lean my head forward and roll my eyes upward, I can see *some* of the top of my head in the glass in front of me, but I can't see all of it. I wouldn't want to. Some valiant few hairs are holding on up there, but I lament their lost brothers, no matter that God has them accounted for. I count it a blessing that I am 6'5"; most people look up to instead of down on me. Atop Adriana's brother's head we find a zig-zag scar, remnant of an operation he underwent at two months to remove a prematurely fused section of his skull. Whenever he gets a haircut his teachers ask Karina and me what happened. Or they make cracks about the barber's slipping clippers.

In any case, essays such as this are best accomplished "off the top of one's head," without too much planning or proving, like the acrobatics Adriana and I perform some evenings, after *Jeopardy!*: I lie on the floor, she comes running, I grab her shoulders, kick up her legs; we twist as she flies overhead, a mess of loose hair and giggles, yet she is grace itself, from launch to landing, again and again until bedtime, when I tuck her in with a kiss on the top of her head.

Of course, I've seen the top of her head since the day she was born, and even now, because I am nearly twice her height, when we go walking, I see the top of her head when I glance down. It is a father's perspective. Or a god's.

When Thomas Higginson asked Emily Dickinson to define poetry, she wrote, "If I feel physically as if the top of my head were taken off, I know that is poetry." I am a father. I feel that every single day.

Old Time Rock and Roll
(feat. Michael Martone)

One afternoon when I was fifteen or so, I sat in the parking lot of the Broadmoor Theatre in Bill Bartol's car. We'd just watched *Space Camp*, as I recall, which was probably the first time I recognized "camp" not simply as the location of summer youth activities but as an aesthetic category. Spurred by Bill's more mature vision of the film, I had cheered raucously when the kids solved the orbital problem and made their way safely back to earth (after an unfortunate accident launched their simulator into space? is that what happened?). But I have brought us to this moment not to expound upon the various ways we interpret and thereby understand art, or lack thereof, but to revisit a serendipitous event that returns and resonates with me often, though thirty years have intervened.

You're expecting some narrative of that moment, I presume, but first allow me a bit of background, some character development. Bill and I were schoolmates and bandmates at Catholic High School in downtown Baton Rouge. I was a freshman and he was a senior. I played trombone and he played baritone, which meant we often played the same parts, me with a slide and he with valves. He drove his own car and lived near me in the eastern subdivision called Sherwood Forest. I suppose we shared more than geography and music, probably a sense of humor, and certainly Bill was kind and generous with his time. I was new to the school and to the city, having recently moved from New Jersey when my father got an assignment at the Exxon refinery on the Mississippi, so I was grateful for his friendship. In any case, Bill and I would sometimes drive to our band conductor's apartment, mostly to give him a hard time and listen to jazz, which they loved and I tried to love, in order to fit in. Bill had lots of Pink Floyd records, which he'd sometimes play, and which I also tried to "get" in order to be cool. Pink Floyd had entered my life years earlier, in New Jersey, when the older kids down the street decided to drop KISS in favor of the angsty psychedelia of *The Wall* (I benefited from their decision, inheriting several albums, though not *Hotter Than Hell*, which I refused, worrying that its title and starry-nippled woman on the cover would upset my mother). One day I was at Bill's house when a hurricane made landfall. We decided to play basketball in his driveway. The water quickly rose to almost knee-level, so we couldn't dribble, but we had a blast shooting against the whipping wind.

Speaking of against the wind, let's return to that moment in Bill's car outside the Broadmoor Theatre. I can no longer recall any prelude (other than the campy movie, which, I've learned, starred Kelly Preston, Lea Thompson, and Joaquin Phoenix), so I'll just tell you that just before he cranked the key to start the engine, Bill and I simultaneously and without prompting began to sing "Don't try to take me to a disco!" from Bob Seger's "Old Time Rock & Roll." Even as we sang we laughed with wonder at the coincidence, the sheer unlikelihood of hitting upon the same verse of the same song with no discernible external prompting. As I recall, we'd even begun on the same note. I've never been much of a Bob Seger fan, and I don't think Bill was either, and this was eight years after the song's release (three years after its rebirth in *Risky Business*, which I've still never seen).

We remarked on the strangeness of the moment and sought proximate causes but found none. We hadn't been listening to the radio; the song hadn't appeared in the movie. Neither of us could remember the last time we'd heard it, nor could we express the motivation we'd felt to belt it out (beginning, we should note, in the middle of the first verse). While it's true that neither of us enjoyed disco, our aversion hadn't been a topic of conversation.

Isn't that cool/weird? I certainly think so, and I've carried the occasion with me across decades, wondering what it might mean, or *whether* it might mean anything, even wondering if I might have modified the happening in memory, increasing its strangeness. Given my continued preference for classic rock, my continued reliance on FM radio for my driving soundtrack, and the continued popularity of Seger's best-loved song, my mind is cast back to this event often.

But I've never written of it before. So here I wonder: What place does an anecdote like this have within contemporary culture, or why should it occasion an essay now, thirty-odd years after the fact (when the accumulation of memories has certainly clouded the clarity we must have felt then)? What significance does the moment contain, or reveal? Why bother sharing it with others?

This is the part where the essay veers, requires both my and your consciousnesses to care and to make something of the past. Perhaps this is an exploration of memory and the things that stick, however tenuously, or the things that seem to matter, simply as a result of their longevity. Or perhaps their longevity signals their importance. Perhaps it's a single data point in the debate about free will or the law of large numbers, which deflates the magic we feel at strange coincidences, clarifying that every unlikely event was bound to happen to someone somewhere. Perhaps it's a lament at the loss of common culture, even pop culture, even formulized and manipulated culture, wherein an artless mogul waits to see which song catches a bit of a wave, then pumps it into all available outlets, ensuring its growth and popularity and return on investment, until it becomes part of the masses' subconscious, always primed to burst forth in idle moments. Perhaps it's not a lament but a sigh of relief, for those same reasons. And perhaps it's a worry that with individualized playlists and earbuds in every ear, we're no longer paying attention to what anyone else is singing aloud, no longer allowing songs to live much beyond their moment, as they're piped directly into our ears, and that a kid like me, uprooted in adolescence and transplanted far from home, might never find a friend who can drive and share music and guffaw at ridiculous plot twists and shoot hoops in the raging rain.

Vehicular Vehicles

A definition of coincidence is the occupation of the same area of space or happening at the same time. Sixteen years ago, I totaled my car in an accident at the intersection of Paul W. Bryant Boulevard and Twenty-third Avenue in Tuscaloosa. I was okay, but the airbags in my 1996 Honda deployed, filling the cabin with a foul-smelling powder I mistook for smoke from a fire (the bags are packed in cornstarch so they won't stick when folded up) as I plowed into the white, late-model Buick that had run a stop sign and was suddenly in front of me. The day before, my then sixteen-year-old son, Sam, had gotten his license, had driven that night—his first solo and uneventful mission in this now very totaled auto. "A delicious irony" is all he said when I told him he now no longer had his ride.

This wasn't my first automobile accident. My life in high school was a series of accidents. Life in high school perhaps is a series of accidents. Life itself is perhaps a series of accidents. In high school, as I attempted to make a left-hand turn, a car skidded into me. I watched it in the mirror and had enough time to think, "Hold on," before I was hit. Again in high school, I pirouetted at seventy on a patch of black ice near Marion, Indiana, on I-69. And again in high school, I was able to destroy both family cars simultaneously when, shifting the Camaro into drive, I got stuck in reverse and slammed into the Cutlass parked behind it.

Teaching the narrative essay to my freshman comp class years ago at Iowa State University, I had to issue a blanket prohibition on the subject. No writing about one's car accidents. There were so many, and my students took, I think, these dramatic coincidences as the natural occasion to retell, primed for narrative treatment, a story ready to be told. But in most cases, in cases that even involved a death or deaths, the experience had not altered the world of its narrator in any meaningful way. Their accidents, reconstructed in such loving and exact detail, had not engendered any profound change in their behaviors, had not led them to a conscience-altering revelation about the meaning of life or death. Those accidents had not even stopped them from hopping into the next car to come along, to take off down the same tragic and now morbidly attractive and compellingly dangerous section of road as their recent mishap. Thinking about the accident, or more precisely, the writing about the accident, if it did anything at all to their psyches, only conjured within them the cool sensation of the event, the rush of dumb luck. Their lives, by virtue of accident, became interesting, but the accident was not a propellant onto a different plane, an altered state.

I hopped into my new car bought with insurance money. I noticed I was still skittish at intersections, and the accident made for a good anecdote. The detail about the cornstarch and the airbags is a particularly attractive embellishment, I believe. A wreck feels like it should be the vehicle to some climactic revelation. And who knows? Perhaps things were set in motion in my life all those years ago by the coincidence of two cars inhabiting the same space and time. It would be a good story but I would need to imagine the true vectors of the collision, the physics of consequence not coincidence.

The Arrogance of Style

MOST OF THE WORLD'S SQUABBLES ARE
OCCASIONED BY GRAMMAR!
—MONTAIGNE

1. Never use "comma-then" in literary writing.

When crafting complex sentences, avoid following a comma with the word *then* introducing a dependent or a relative clause, unless you want *New Yorker* regular and bestselling writer Jonathan Franzen to accuse you of "not listening to the English language when you're writing." Thus do not write,

> I read a Jonathan Franzen polemic on the Farrar, Straus and Giroux website, then wrote a comment rebutting one of Franzen's key claims.

If you believe that you *do* in fact listen to the English language, perhaps you are simply an unwitting product of MFA culture. According to Franzen, "No native speaker would utter [a comma-then phrase], except in a creative-writing class." Thus eschew,

> Franzen begins his diatribe invoking the worn cliché about "so many ____, so little time" (in this case, it's "so much to read"), then snides into specifics with "one of the best reasons a writer can give me [to put a book down] is to use the word *then* as a conjunction without a subject following it."

**2. Except if you follow "comma-then"
with an independent clause(?).**

Franzen allows for this seemingly arbitrary exception, explaining that before independent clauses, *then* functions as an adverb, not as a conjunction. Native speakers, he claims, are okay with this, too. Thus you might continue your narrative with:

> My first encounter with the comma-then "rule" came during the copyediting of my second book, during which Jeremy Hall noted the "problem" in the following sentence: "Peter stopped and explained, 'You collect the spit in the front of your mouth, then you tighten your lips, clench your teeth, and push your tongue forward so the spit squeezes through the space between your front teeth.'" He said "Adverbial in nature, *then* should not technically operate as a conjunction in this fashion."

As alluded to above, this particular example includes a subject following *then* ("then *you* tighten your lips"); thus Franzen would allow it.

> But Jeremy Hall would not, at least initially. Basing his argument on the fact that *then* is not one of the FANBOYS (a mnemonic to remember *all* viable coordinating conjunctions: *for, and, nor, but, or, yet, so*), and that it can be moved around in a sentence without losing meaning ("you then tighten your lips," "you tighten, then, your lips," "you tighten your lips then") while true coordinating conjunctions cannot (go ahead; try it), he deemed my sentence ungrammatical. Along with many others in the book.

3. Well, if you're by nature more of a descriptive grammarian than a prescriptivist, then push back.

Perhaps you believe, either passionately or vaguely, that the English language has developed the way it has over long years as a kind of negotiation among millions of speakers from myriad backgrounds and societies and statuses, some of whom are educated in the niceties of grammar, most of whom are not, and that even the prescriptivists are not tapped into the mind of God on the matter. They began with an already evolved language and attempted to exert influence on it, to shape it and standardize it, and they've certainly had some success, but the language keeps on making its own sense via unruly speakers and writers who care not a whit whether their conjunctive adverb is a FANBOY or whatever.

> To his credit, Jeremy had also noted the "smug/arrogant tone" of the Franzen diatribe, which he had consulted independently, and when pressed on the issue, he agreed to a compromise, with me stetting about half of my comma-thens, "not killing [my] darlings at the expense of [my] voice, but perhaps keeping them in check with measured usage," as he said.

That example doesn't even include a comma-then or any other "clever" dig at the "rules." So are we done here?

4. For the sake of your mental health, just let it go.

Otherwise, you might end up spending an inordinate amount of time researching such a minuscule, insignificant, easily resolved issue, bothering your more-grammatical friends, asking of them time and insights far beyond the merits of your one-way feud with a faraway famous writer whose tone has rankled you. Thus please do not report:

> I asked my old editor boss, Andrew Olsen, what he thought. He replied that he often used comma-then, "which tells how I feel about it," and he "asked a colleague, Jake Frandsen, to see what the Corpus of Contemporary American English (COCA) shows about the construction. He found that [, then] had 68,595 hits (mostly in fiction), and [, and then] had only 15,446 hits. So the construction that Jonathan Franzen objects to is preferred 82% of the time in that corpus."

> My colleague Brian Jackson astutely pointed out that Franzen's okay example "I sang a couple of songs, then Katie got up and sang a few herself," would by Franzen's own argument be a comma splice (given that both phrases include subject and verb, and *then* is not a coordinating conjunction), yet Franzen allows it for "propulsive effect"?).

My recently retired colleague Kristine Hansen went above and beyond in her response to my query, researching widely but primarily in the *Longman Grammar of Spoken and Written English* (London: Pearson, 1999) and writing me a two-thousand-word letter full of detailed examples and explanations. Based on Biber et al.'s analysis of a forty-million-word corpus of American and British texts, Hansen discovered that "some of the adverbial uses of *then* are very much like the uses of conjunctions." She points out that *then* is the most common time adverbial, which we already kind of know instinctively, and we can understand comma-then in this sense/function, but *then* is also a "linking adverbial," which, according to the *Longman Grammar,* is used to "make semantic connections between spans of discourse of varying length," those connections including "enumeration and addition, summation, apposition, result/inference, contrast/concession, and transition." Any number of these functions could be seen as justification for a comma-then clause. While linking adverbials differ from coordinating conjunctions in their flexible positioning (as demonstrated above: they can be moved without losing meaning), they nevertheless can perform in the position where one might usually supply an *and,* and in fact they "don't have to be used with a conjunction." Hansen concludes that "As it conveys a sequence of events, *then* not only expresses a meaning of time, but also serves a cohesive function." Frankly, the more I learn about *then,* the more impressed I get.

This all seems a little technical for descriptivist grammar, but thank you for bothering your colleagues in the pursuit of truth. I believe we can all rest easy now, knowing that the question is settled once and for all. As your colleague Kristine Hansen said, "If there is one true statement that can be made about language, it is that it is always changing. What we consider correct is purely a matter of convention and sometimes a matter of prejudice."

5. So . . . perhaps we might say: Don't make absolute claims about other writers' practices without even bothering to check if you're right.

For instance, if you happen to respect Charles Dickens and the Brontë sisters, and/or think that they represent a bygone era of quality writing, and/or think that your readers will recognize your name-check and accept your premise without question based on the ethos of these canonical novelists, and/or think who's got time to reread all those long novels anyway, please remember that all of these texts are in the public domain and are easily searchable. Thus beware:

> I read Franzen's claim that "Dickens and the Brontës got along fine without comma-then," then went straight to Project Gutenberg to find out, then wrote a comment on the FSG site, saying "Just for fun, I just took about 5 minutes to do the most basic of searches on Gutenberg.org to see if Dickens and the Brontës ever employed comma-then in just the way Franzen forbids. Oh yes they did. Quite a lot. ['Uriah kept it up a little while, then sent it back to Mrs. Heep.' / 'I listened doubtingly an instant; detected the disturber, then turned and dozed.']"

6. Fascinating.

So Franzen tried to bolster his argument by claiming that Dickens and the Brontës were on his side, but they're actually not?

Yep.

And it's untrue that comma-then is "an irritating, lazy mannerism . . . that occurs almost exclusively in 'literary' writing of the past few decades"?

Yep.

7. What happened next?

Did Franzen respond? Anyone from FSG?

My comment got dozens of upvotes or thumbs up or likes or whatever, and several other commenters similarly argued convincingly against the comma-then prohibition, then FSG removed all comments from their website.

Again, that's one of those Franzen-approved "propulsive effect" sentences, no? Do you think the decision to remove commenting from the site was a direct result of your comment?

Who can say?

8. Well, we certainly *can* say go ahead and use comma-then in literary writing.

Dickens and the Brontës did it; so can you! Do you have more examples?

Do I!? I may have to add an appendix to hold them, and I'm not even convinced that I've gotten them all (though I've been quite thorough). It's worth admitting, for the sake of fairness and full disclosure, that Anne Brontë alone among our four forebears seems to agree with Franzen. She never wrote comma-then in *The Tenant of Wildfell Hall* or *Agnes Gray*, though she used comma-and-then over a hundred times.

And yet?

And yet . . .

The Pickwick Papers (1836):
"Like a gas-lamp in the street, with the wind in the pipe, he had exhibited for a moment an unnatural brilliancy, then sank so low as to be scarcely discernible; after a short interval, he had burst out again, to enlighten for a moment; then flickered with an uncertain, staggering sort of light, and then gone out altogether."

Oliver Twist (1837):
"Oliver involuntarily shrunk back, and then laughed at himself for being so foolish, then cried, then laughed again . . ."

Nicholas Nickleby (1838):
"His hopeful friend and pupil drew a chair to the breakfast-table, and essayed to eat; but, finding that impossible, lounged to the window, then loitered up and down the room with his hand to his fevered head . . ."

The Old Curiosity Shop (1840):
"This done, she begged them in a kind of deep despair to drink; then laughed, then cried, then took a little sip herself, then laughed and cried again, and took a little more."

Jane Eyre (1847):
"I took that dear hand, held it a moment to my lips, then let it pass round my shoulder."

Wuthering Heights (1848):
"He laid them on the table, looked eagerly towards the window, then rose and went out."

David Copperfield (1849):
"Dora left off shaking her curls, and laid her trembling little hand upon my shoulder, and first looked scared and anxious, then began to cry."

Bleak House (1852):
"Jo searches the floor for some time longer, then looks up for a moment, and then down again."

Great Expectations (1860):
"Joe looked at her in a helpless way, then took a helpless bite . . ."

. . . and those are just one example each from only about half the books.

Okay! Okay! Uncle! I'm convinced. And grateful for the lesson. But we seem to have strayed from our original purpose to instruct and edify writers. How about we end with an old, inoffensive classic? Such as . . .

9. Omit needless words.

Gotcha. Like the whole of Jonathan Franzen's fulmination? And maybe this entire rejoinder?

Yep.

Distance (feat. Joni Tevis)

Looking to the majestic mountain in front of us, Rory said, "This is when Timpanogos looks like a postcard," and I thought, as I often do, how the stillness is an illusion of distance, how if we were standing on one of its peaks, we'd be whipped and blown by cold winds, and what tree branches we saw would be all in motion. I thought of the stilling effect of distance and said something to that effect, feeling as I said it that I was grasping at the rough shape of an essay I might discover if I began to write it. Rory agreed, adding, "It's just like the Bette Midler song 'From a Distance.' You know? She talks about how everything looks tranquil *from a distance*" (he sang that last titular bit). Of course she does, I thought, and confirmed the lyrical message later. "From a distance," she croons with aching earnestness, everything is peace and plenty, there's no poverty, no violence, there's friendship instead of war, and God looks on . . . it's not clear how: contented? clueless? disappointed? testing us?

I have discovered time and again that what original thought I thought I had thought was long ago thought better and expressed more eloquently by another thinker more intelligent and more elegant, and always I've accepted my overlap humbly, feeling that at least I have happened down the same path as one of the greats. But when I learned that Bette Midler, or (later, upon confirming the lyrics) that songwriter Julie Gold beat me to the notion of distance's quelling influence and used it to make a Grammy-winning, multi-platinum-selling, music box–filling, Congressional Record–entering, Mir Space Station–alarming, children's-book/calendar/greeting-card-inspiring, tear-jerking, heart-touching pop song, well . . .

Titanium White. Prussian Blue. Sap Green.

He films on a simple set, wearing simple clothes—jeans, button-front shirt, a chest pocket from which a gray squirrel, Peapod, sometimes emerges. He can make a painting, start to finish, in an unhurried twenty-four minutes. Once or twice an episode he slaps his brush against the easel leg with a quick authority that I love. "You figured it out," he says. "I just like to clean the brush."

In 1990, when Bette Midler released her version of "From a Distance," Bob Ross was teaching painters to create the illusion of distance by blurring the bases of trees or mountains in the middle of his canvases. "Don't want too much detail," he murmurs. "The lack of detail helps create that illusion of distance . . . little things are happening back in the distance."

He'd started painting landscapes while stationed at Eielson Air Force Base, south of Fairbanks, Alaska, using a wet-on-wet technique that allowed him to finish a piece during breaks between shifts. In an interview with the Orlando Sentinel *in 1991, Ross reflected that, as a first sergeant, "I was the guy who makes you scrub the latrine, the guy who makes you make your bed, the guy who screams at you for being late to work. The job requires you to be a mean, tough person. And I was fed up with it. I promised myself that if I ever got away from it, it wasn't going to be that way any more." So in his show, he's soft-spoken, narrating the process as though he's explaining it to just one person, just to me. I like the way the names of the paints run across the bottom of the screen (*DARK SIENNA, PHTHALO BLUE, CADMIUM YELLOW*) as he manages to pull foreground, middle ground, and background from his canvas by smudging the paint while wet. "The mist becomes the separator, becomes your best friend," he says. "Cherish it, take care of it."*

His love for painting woos me. "Tell you what, tell you what," he says. "Thought we'd just have some fun." And it is fun, all of it: thumb hooked through his big Plexiglas palette, he blends paint with a blunt knife, loads the blade with pigment, scratches branch lines onto the wet canvas, knocks excess thinner out of yet another two-inch brush. "Beat the devil out of it," he says, laughing. "That really is the fun part." As a line of alpenglow-lit mountains rears against the winter sky. As a cabin made of weathered wood asserts itself beside a copse of birches. "See how you can change your mind?" he says. "That easy."

"And off we go."

Beat on the Brat

The spark was a kid in downtown Colón, Montevideo, wearing a Ramones T-shirt featuring the lyrics "Beat on the brat with a baseball bat," which song I'd never heard, not being much into punk, especially in my formative years. So I've just listened. It's typical Ramones, if I am qualified to judge, having heard only a few of their songs on the radio: eighth-note strumming atop a steady high-hat, bass-drum, snare downbeat, punctuated by simple flourishes and lots of crash cymbal. Joey Ramone sounds a bit more British than I've known him to be, but his languid, laconic vocals are unmistakable. The song contains only twenty-one unique words, including "oh yeah," but not "oh-ho," which would make it twenty-two, I guess? How did these guys ever become cool? I wonder. Certainly their affect is nothing like the glaring menace of coolness in my high school.

A glimmer of hope: even the nerds and dweebs sometimes find a place.

I say "spark," because the saying on the shirt called to my memory a brief friend, Andy, complaining at the Beastie Boys' similar expression of violence, from "Posse in Effect," off 1986's *Licensed to Ill*: "Punk in the hall, man, I shoulda oughta hit him." "Why hit a punk?" Andy wondered. "Punks are cool." Andy considered himself a punk, as in a rebel, a listener to angsty, cacophonous music, and he thought of the Beastie Boys as the rap arm of punk, which they probably were, having begun their musical forays as a hardcore punk band, before the allure of rap aligned with opportunity and they lucked into fame and fortune. In any case, I was never clear whether "punk" in this context meant a kid like Andy or simply a guy Ad Rock didn't like, punks and brats being conditional categories, subjective statuses, relative to the speaker, and all. We got along well, Andy and I, through our mutual interest in the Boy Scouts, a generally un-punk activity, and the fact that we lived relatively near one another and were both tapped to staff the 1987 Brownsea Leadership Training Camp outside Baton Rouge. Andy had a car, so he drove us there, bounding over hills along a two-lane highway north of the city, blasting the Beasties, recklessly passing in the no-passing zone, so that once, as we crested a ridge in the wrong lane, Andy had to swerve violently to avoid a collision.

We laughed nervously, as I recall, and kept singing along.

Maybe there's nothing to lyrics like those, or maybe they're their own outlet, an escape valve, a way of avoiding the violence they propose. Maybe they're sung in persona to convey the absurdity of bullies (or parents) beating on the weak. Or maybe they're an imagined revenge on those bullies, who really *would* beat on another with a baseball bat. When you're scrawny and shy, your opportunities for real-world retaliation are limited, so maybe the high-speed, high-volume energy of a song is just what you need to feel . . . not so alone, perhaps.

And maybe they're alliteration and rhyme before meaning. *Beat, brat, baseball, bat.* Simple sounds that fit a linguistic pattern, meaning be damned (mostly).

I say "they," but the Beasties' lyrics are not alliterative, not yet rhyming (we have to wait another line for the complementary "bit 'em"), and, notably, the act is never carried out. "I shoulda oughta hit him" performs the literary transformation of the impossible real-world confrontation. The singer (and his audience) can hide in the conditional, experience a bravado release in the song, out of harm's way.

I might also have remembered another line from a Beastie Boys song, had my mind made the associative leap off the bat instead of the beating. This is "Paul Revere," also from the band's first album:

I did it like this, I did it like that, I did it with a wiffle-ball bat

Even in my innocence I understood the absent antecedent. While it's somewhat vague, it's rather too clear, don't you think? I cannot recall how these words affected me then. I believe I sang along (in general, but also that day driving to Camp Avondale, swerving wildly to avoid collision). I believe they did not inspire me, not even to titter.

Now they repulse me.

Especially because a couple of years later, once I'd moved back to New Jersey, two twin brothers I competed against in track and field, from nearby Glen Ridge, did that very thing. With a wiffle-ball bat. To a developmentally disabled girl from their school. After a baseball practice at a park, they, with several teammates, convinced the girl to join them in their basement, where a half dozen of the boys undressed her, encouraged her to perform oral sex, and cheered wildly as she bent over and they penetrated her bodily and with all manner of objects. She had the mental capacity of an eight-year-old. They told her they were her friends. Soon after, she told a teacher that she didn't want to get them in trouble. She had finally made friends with the cool kids. They bragged in the locker room and in the hallways, planned a follow-up assault, which they would film, and within a few weeks, the principal caught wind and called the police. Two kids pled out for reduced sentences in exchange for their testimony against the others. The twin brothers I kind of knew, who even before then had seemed too full of themselves, of swagger, of bluster, were eventually sentenced to seven and fifteen years. The court ruled, repeatedly, that their victim did not have the understanding necessary to stop the attacks.

I did not consider myself a punk; I was not cool. I was a kind of nerd, interested in school, music, sports, reading all sorts of books, obeying my parents; circumspect to a fault. News of the assault spread quickly, and the newspapers published pictures and names, so my friends and I saw our sports rivals the Scherzer brothers, but could not recognize them at all.

The mythos surrounding the Beastie Boys made me uncomfortable even as I continued to listen to their record. Their playing at cool included more than sexist lyrics; their objectification of women manifested in well-documented public statements and actions dismissing women as sex toys, and in scantily clad women dancing in cages at their concerts. To me they seemed, at least in their public personas, to embrace fully the role of stereotypical boy-man, privileged jerk concerned only with his own gratification.

Like a lot of people, I lost track of the Beastie Boys once they were no longer foisted upon me by radio and MTV, so I didn't know of their "enlightenment" until MCA died of cancer at age forty-seven. Newspapers and websites in 2012's culture of compassion were quick to recall how in 1994's "Sure Shot" he'd proffered an "apology" (one, like so many, that othered women as mothers, sisters, wives, and friends, relational terms assuming a man's point of view) and offered his love and respect after noting, in passive voice,

The disrespect to women has got to be through

In other venues, band members have also apologized for homophobic lyrics, saying "Time has healed our stupidity," and MCA has expressed concern about "how what I'm doing affects the rest of the world," and thus used his public persona to speak out against American racism (especially Islamophobia) and misogyny.

Which is a good turn of events, no doubt, but who can track the band's contributions to the problems they later came to recognize and repent of? Who can weigh the debits and the credits? Where are we left in this day, when these now-model citizens (and eulogized giant) could certainly be called to account for their past sexual assaults (not only lyrical, not only performative; there's online video of MCA signing a woman's abdomen then reaching his hand down her pants as she protests).

Perhaps the timing was right to allow for the band's repentance, and surely repentance is better than intransigence. Perhaps the accumulation of their later statements and actions convinces us of their sincerity. Perhaps we recall that such blatant misogyny was considered normal, or it fit into a systemic misogyny, or if it was extreme, we took it as entertainment, not "real life." What I'm trying to say is that I can't explain why the collective we (and I realize that we are not all in agreement; we never are) has given the Beastie Boys a pass, when we've generally come (again?) to view what they represented as morally repugnant. I can't settle, finally, on any particular point of view. I am relieved that they awoke to a kind of empathy with less-fortunate others, and I appreciate their efforts to right their past wrongs, and

I am glad that they've been either forgiven or forgotten enough to find a teachable audience now. I also realize that their first album and its attendant media (videos, interviews, etc.) are still widely available, just a mouse-click away, and likely still hold sway with certain segments of the population (the frat boys, the bros, perhaps even the white supremacists who recently defaced Adam Yauch Park in Brooklyn). And I recognize the difficulty of growing up in public, and I know that I am guilty of my own sins. As Ad Rock said in response to hypocrisy charges, "All you can hope for is change, and I'd rather be a hypocrite . . . than a zombie."

I don't consider myself any kind of expert or sage, either, no one to be listened to

Feeling myself too ill-instructed to instruct others

so I will cut short here, abort the essay before we solve the world's problems, because I do not believe that such solutions exist, and if they do, they will not be found in an obscure essay, so instead, I think I'll give us another memory with Andy, one less fraught with danger:

After one week at the Brownsea camp, he and I took our dirty clothes to the nearest laundromat, where we discovered that the giant dryers could be run with a person inside, if his friend held down the switch to trick the machine into thinking its door was closed. Thus we enjoyed a kind of harmless jolly idiocy for a few moments, crouched in a drum with our feet out the door, spinning fast enough to get dizzy but slow enough to tumble from top to bottom if we didn't hold on. We were young enough that dizziness was still a pleasurable feeling, and might have gone on like this forever, but for the heat: after a revolution or two, the pilot light would spark the gas jets in a flaming whoosh, and the drum would become unbearable. So, soon enough, still swaying with imbalance, we cut it out and just loaded up our wet clothes.

Against the Wind

One afternoon after our lunch break, Elder Gray and I were rushing to get out of the house, and for the first time we shared the bathroom for teeth brushing and hand washing. The bathroom was typical of its kind in Uruguay. It was a small, dark, neglected room at the back of the house with a chipped and worn blue wooden door that hung askew on its hinges and stuck against its frame when it was closed. The room was lit from a small cantilever window high on the back wall and a naked light bulb, whose switch was placed temptingly outside the door in the hallway. The bulb shined dimly from above the stained mirror on the left wall.

I suspect the bathroom may have been designed to save money on materials. Gray tile lined the floor and walls up to a height of about two meters as a protective barrier against the outbursts from the bent pipe sticking out of the wall which we used to bathe ourselves every morning. The shower drain was built directly into the floor, but it didn't get any help from the floor's slant, and there was a long-handled squeegee at hand to nudge the water on its way down the drain and out to the street. The low-rider toilet sat directly in front of the shower pipe, and if it weren't for the plastic electric water heater that capped the pipe and slowed down the water's flow to a peaceful cascade of drips while it heated, you could probably sit on the "water" (that's what they call the toilet in Uruguay; imagine it pronounced *wah-tare*) and do your thing while you were washing your hair. Somebody once told me that the term was a shortening of "water closet," from the English, who developed much of Montevideo. Still, if the word for the john was somewhat of a mystery, its friend and companion, the bidet—same word in Spanish, English, and, of course, French—had obvious origins.

While a bidet might suggest good hygiene and a high-class standard of living, most homes I checked out for this sort of thing had one, but not many were very hygienic or luxurious. The bidet's popularity, though, probably had an adverse effect on the toilet paper industry in the country, and all we could usually find were raspy greenish-brown rolls that, we joked, must have been made from tree bark. I rarely used the bidet in the homes I lived in, preferring a good chafing to the unfamiliar. Mostly I had fiddled around with them just to see what the experience was like, and I ended up using the toilet paper to dry my rear end after the washing anyway. I never questioned how other people might dry themselves off, and never imagined they might not use the toilet paper.

When he was done spitting his toothpaste lather into the sink, Elder Gray graciously stepped aside and I began to wash my hands. Another architectural annoyance in the bathroom was that the sink faucet was extremely short and barely extended past the sink's edge, affording no room for your hands under the water. But by now I had learned to contort my fingers and direct the stream outward from the edge, and I could wash quickly and enjoyably. I lathered up as best I could with the cold water and hard soap and decided to wash my face too. The lather nearly disappeared as my hands rubbed across my brow and cheeks, but the water was cool and refreshing, and at least it rinsed away some of the morning's sweat. Then I threw meager handfuls of water on my face with my right hand while I held my tie in my left to keep it from slipping into the sink. When whatever soap I had gotten on me was rinsed off, I made a habitual grab for the landlady's old green towel that was always hanging across the room on a rack. I perfunctorily dried my hands and as I lifted the towel to my face I heard a gasp and a surprised, "No way!" I continued my motion and swept the towel quickly from forehead to chin, then looked up to see what was the matter. Some delinquent water gathered on the tip of my nose and I tried to blow it off. Before I could ask, "What?" Elder Gray asked, "You use that towel to dry your *face*?" with such an emphasis on the word *face* that I knew something was up. "Yeah,"

I answered casually. I couldn't guess what was wrong. He continued, in disbelief, "That's the towel for the *bidet!*"

I can't tell if most missionaries figure that sort of thing out for themselves, or if somebody else tells them earlier on, but I froze and stared at the towel for a second and for the first time noticed its grungy discolorations and its position right next to the bidet. Suddenly it all made sense. Elder Gray was telling the truth, and I felt so stupid for never having realized it before. My mind flew back to every house I had yet lived in in Uruguay. In every home the story was the same. There was a landlady; a traditional, old Uruguayan woman whom I never saw buy toilet paper; there was a bidet next to the toilet in the bathroom; and there was a towel hanging constantly right next to that. I cringed to think of all the times I had washed my face and dried it off.

But at the same time, I realized that this was another case of "what you don't know won't hurt you." Before the unfortunate realization, I never noticed any problems in my complexion and was never able to smell my own face. The knowledge of the towel's purpose had somehow worked retroactively and turned my stomach for all those times I had unwittingly contaminated my face. But I never knew it then. So, while I certainly stopped drying my face with the towel that was meant for my butt, I felt a little, in a petty way, like Bob Seger, running against the wind and singing "I wish I didn't know now what I didn't know then."

Pangram Haiku

Pangrams use all the
letters, give quick wisdom, fix
our banjaxed vizards

Haiku require a
wonder, but context zips by
in fog, like veiled jam

Essays juxtapose
mundane and queer, believe the
weight, reck the fazing

Together, they smile
quizzically, wax joking, for
pablum dims our vim

Whenever I most
yearn for luck, God jinxes my
bequest, picks my maze

Extra wisdom feels
boring, each jerk of pique lives,
every wink a zero

Amazed by vext words
I check joyful meaning and
improv equally

Whenever I judge,
the jackalope zigs, zags, zooms
beyond the faux quale

Alphabetize your
karma, sever your qigong,
jinx your wifi code

Whenever I laze
about, my quick wit fades, my
jeux d'esprit agley

Required to write so
vexingly, I ambush these
mere frowzy jackpots

Whenever I fix
my quips to the jazzy world,
I come back agape

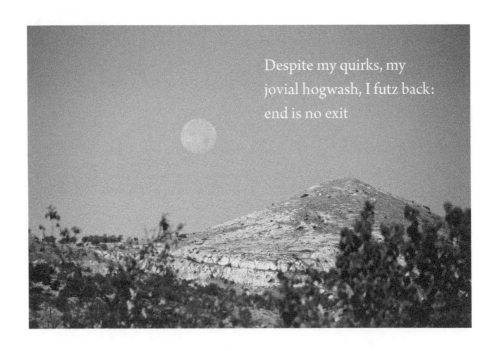

Despite my quirks, my
jovial hogwash, I futz back:
end is no exit

Plums (feat. Matthew Gavin Frank)

Here is a memory: Elder Solomon and I standing on ladders and sitting on branches in the plum trees in Lemes's yard in Paysandú. The sun warms and the breeze cools, toward a wavering equilibrium, suggesting that all is right in the world. Lemes is the branch president of the Mormons in the northeast, mostly rural, quadrant of the city. His first name may be Juan, though I don't really remember. Nor do I remember his wife and children, not really, though he *was* married, as I recall. This must be early autumn, so, April, we'll say, in this the Southern Hemisphere. I think we have stopped by unannounced and unanticipated to find Lemes (and family) harvesting their plums, and so, like all missionaries everywhere, fatigued of being a nuisance and always keen to be of service, we have clambered into the branches with buckets and bags. We laugh and share stories. We talk about missionary work in the branch. We give updates on our investigators, primarily Teresita and José, whom I inherited when I arrived last December, a month before Elder Solomon, and about whom I still know so little, but that they're living in a shed and raising chickens. Teresita is pregnant, precariously, as she's miscarried before, so she's on bed rest, but she's often up and about, shuffling not hustling, but still. I think José does changas and Teresita may sometimes make pasteles to sell to the neighbors. They were married last month, which was our doing, given that our church won't baptize them if their union is not properly authorized by the local bureaucracy. They were okay with this, mind, but it was we missionaries who made the arrangements downtown, and it was the local members who baked a cake and brought gifts and bought a lilac dress for Teresita. José forgot to shave. He wore an unbuttoned button-down shirt. None of their extended family attended. Somewhere I have a curling photo of José hunched over signing the marriage register, Teresita looking on smiling, Solomon (in all his glory) raising an eyebrow as if to underscore the cultural differences between his neatly ordered life back in Utah and this.

And what is *this*, exactly?

This, friends, is an essay, a translation of memory into words and an attempt to find something of significance without preaching, which, truth be told, was our missionary charge, preaching was, more so than picking plums to help someone who didn't really need our help. But Lemes accepted it graciously and perhaps with relief that he could get rid of some, sending us on our way with a plastic bagful. Isn't that always the problem? Timing and distribution? If trees produced their fruits regularly and evenly, there would be no waste, no rot, and we would always be sated.

But *this*, back then, was two people within an economic system so harsh (and so cold) that they struggled to provide for their most basic necessities. This was a child on the way, fated to a difficult life, faced from birth with challenges I'd never had to overcome. This was Teresita's lisp and slow speech, José's stares into the distance. Also an openness, a humility so sweet, so guileless. The stumps we sat on in the yard as we read from the Book of Mormon and answered questions, as the chickens pecked and fluttered. Somewhere I have a curling photo of me hunched over my triple combination, page opened to somewhere in 3 Nephi, I would suppose, smiling wryly at the camera, glancing sidelong at the white chicken perched on my arm.

Soon, amidst our contented conversation, our methodical picking and putting away, the sun dropped low across the river, past Colón, past San José. Solomon and I had had our fill of plums, they were delicious, and we wondered if we'd eat them all before they went bad. We hopped on our bikes, strapped on our helmets, and kicked off, the plastic bag of plums dangling from my handlebars, beating a chaotic staccato against my front fork. Our route home took us past Teresita and José's shed, so we decided to knock and cast in of our abundance. It's true that they needed food. Yet it is also true that I cannot recall ever bringing them food before this moment of convenience. We brought them memorized lessons, mostly, and checkups. How was the reading going? Would they be attending church this Sunday? When no one answered our knock, we left the bag hanging from their door handle, no note, no anything. We smiled, imagining their surprised gratitude. Though they might suspect, we would not claim the good deed; we would remain anonymous.

Forgive me, I want to say now.

> Forgive me for forgetting that a full plastic bag dangling from a doorknob can, in this light, be a ghost. I'm not saying that this is the ghost of my great-grandmother Sarah, and I'm not saying that when the wind stirs the bag, and one tight plum squeaks against another, that the sound is the sound of her voice, speaking, again, a slurred Yiddish proverb into my six-year-old mother's ear. Sarah's husband had been buried last November, and Sarah had just had her second stroke, and Sarah had sworn off things like stone fruit, because her mouth would no longer cooperate with the skin. So many things,

that summer, were left to rot in a porcelain bowl. In her humid tenement, in Borough Park, Brooklyn, she used my mother again as a dressmaker's dummy. The taffeta was crunchy, the cotton soft. Sarah kept her family afloat sewing clothes for wealthier neighbors. According to Yiddish superstition, she compelled my mom to hold a small bit of bread in her mouth during the entire tailoring process, so that Sarah's own failing hands would not slip and stick my mom's skin with her pins. As long as my mom held that bread on her tongue, she would remain unstuck. And she did, she held it there as it soaked up her saliva, reverted to some horrible dough. She held it there as the plums died. Forgive me also for this imposition. It is not so hot where I live, and I have been inside for days. This blizzard has compelled me toward these memories, and the mailman has fallen against the drifts delivering the box of fruit to my door. My mother sends mail-order oranges, as if from another time. I will take them inside before they freeze. Again, today, I will not take my life, before napping. The dream I will have will have nothing to do with absolution.

I awake, residually tired but comfortable, thousands of miles and days from Paysandú, pull on my slippers and shuffle about in the quiet house, descend the stairs, round the corner, open the cupboards and refrigerator, pour a bowl of cereal for breakfast. In quiet moments I sometimes recall Teresita and José, wonder idly about them, revisit in hazy summary our briefly overlapping lives, feel a tug of fellow-feeling (I will call it, though no words I can find seem to fit), as I resist what I would call *pity*. I can't even remember their last names, and I am sure there is no way to find them now, short of returning to Paysandú and asking around. They would not be on Facebook. They didn't even have a phone. Teresita was baptized. José was not, I don't think. Their daughter was born prematurely and with severe disabilities. I visited them after I was transferred to another area. Perhaps I visited several times. I no longer recall. They were glad to see me, it seemed, and we acted as if all were right in the world. I skirt the edges of wondering just who needed saving, believing such reductions and reversals too thin to hold the weight of my thought.

But these moments of memory and contemplation are rare. As you read of it, you were probably half caught up in the idea-scene, half skeptical of it. The truth is, I am not now eating my breakfast; it is near lunchtime, on a Friday in early December, and there is snow on the ground outside. I am sitting in my office, surrounded by books, typing at my computer, having just written the word *computer* (now again, in italics). *This* is an essay, a document of recollected past experiences and extrapolated present interpretations. I began writing it weeks ago, spurred by a flash of memory: gathering Lemes's plums, leaving them for Teresita and José. I didn't know why this memory returned nor where writing from it might take me, which connections I might uncover and which ideas I might discover.

Another memory returns to me now: Mostly we sat outside in the shade, but once I peeked inside the shed and saw the lumpy bed, the whole-year calendar pinned to the wall, the plywood table, the pair of spindly chairs, the icebox, the whole place orderly and dignified, each spare item arranged and cared for. Teresita and José didn't let on about their dire situation, so that I often wondered if they realized it, by which I mean not just "were aware" of it, but, from the Spanish, if they "made it real." Perhaps the problems I saw didn't exist, because they went unrecognized as such. That season when Solomon and I visited every few days, taught our lessons, asked our questions, sat on stumps hunched over scriptures among the trees and the chickens that were in the yard, our reality was not Teresita and José's reality, I believe now. The plums we left dangling from the door handle disappeared from our view, and while I can imagine that Teresita and José found them, appreciated them, ate them, were nourished and pleased, I never heard about them. To my recollection, they never mentioned the plums or figured out that we'd left them. This was as it should have been, though I suspect now that in my immaturity I felt cheated of the credit. The anticlimax was not then satisfying, though now it is.

I have eaten many plums since, mostly without sparking any memories or regrets, mostly without realizing a connection to my past fraught gesture. But a memory may arrive of its own accord, it seems, without warning, without apparent cause, and leave us silent as its vibrations resound in harmony with our whole unfinished lives, necessitating an essay, which itself will not finish anything either. This is just to say that nothing is simple; nothing is finished; nothing is alone.

Solstice

I have seen forty-seven summer solstices before this one, a few before my memory kicked in and the rest subsumed into a general "cotton wool," as Virginia Woolf called the bulk of life, from which I cannot recall even one particular moment, despite this being a significant day, not in the impositional sense of so many days declared such by humankind (the first of January, the fourth of July), nor in the personal sense of those days important to me (my birthday, my wedding anniversary), but in the astronomical sense, which, despite the date's nomenclature (for Juno, queen of gods) and the numbering (the twenty-first earthly revolution since . . . ? an arbitrary beginning), suggests a leaning toward order beyond our paltry attempts at organizing life.

By writing it, or from it, during and after it, I will fix a small part of it, "it" being my experience of the day, the overlap between my sensory apprehension and the infinite buzzing external reality, and thus I will remember it, or store it somewhere I can return to it and thus call it back again in the future, pretending to remember.

This is my naïve notion: that on some future day I will want to revisit this day, that I will feel proud or relieved or accomplished that I have saved something particular, that despite my shaky recollection I can locate a past self among specific past events. For instance:

- I awoke to my alarm at 5:40, dressed in exercise clothes, woke my sons to get ready for Cub Scout camp, carried the new puppy downstairs and took him outside, encouraging him to pee, which he did.

- After dropping Marcos and James off at the church, I fell asleep on the couch watching Australia play Denmark in the World Cup (the game ended in a 1–1 tie) while the puppy dozed in the corner of the kitchen.

- I awoke to a knock on the door; it was Scott Sullivan, a sprinkler repairman who loves Notre Dame, my alma mater, and who proudly showed me the interlaced ND tattoo on his right biceps then got to work replacing and adjusting and tweaking.

- I exercised not once but twice, in a final sprint toward winning a month-long weight-loss challenge I'd been having with my friends Andrew and Kelly, which was to end the next day. (I played DVDs from Shaun T's *Focus T25* series: Upper Focus and Lower Focus.)

- I watched Argentina lose to Croatia, 3–0, and felt a slight bit of schadenfreudish glee, I admit, though I know many fine Argentinians, and I feel bad for rooting against their team. Nevertheless I do, mostly because I have lived in and loved Uruguay, my wife's home country, and because Argentina is much bigger than Uruguay, and Croatia, and sometimes their national team players can get big-headed and dismissive of other countries, especially Uruguay.

- I took a short walk to the nearest church to spin a Pokéstop for the phone game Pokémon Go, hoping to get a "gift," which I could give to other people who play the game, but I was disappointed, as the rollout was only for players at a higher level than I.

- In preparation for the arrival of Karina's family next week, I cleaned our downstairs office, which had become a storage room for junk we don't know where to put. Mostly I threw things away or recycled them or shuttled them into boxes with lids so I could hide them.

- I sat on a stool at the kitchen island and wrote, mostly staring idly out the back window at the unpredictable movements of the leaves on the peach trees and the illusory stillness of a sliver of mountain visible past the shed we made a few years ago.

- With my whole family, I went to Provo to celebrate the wedding of our friends the Bangerters' oldest son, Tanner, who looks quite a bit like his bride, Sarah, and whose reception featured a live jazz band and delicious homemade cupcakes but not enough time to catch up with Neal and Lee, who had recently moved to London, so we sat in chairs on the lawn and enjoyed the atmosphere and chatted a while with Mary Anne McFarland, mostly about our oldest children, who had both begun missions last September in Mexico right when a series of earthquakes hit.

There was more, of course, including some sleep on either end of the day, and some meals, and bathroom breaks, about which nobody wants to hear, not even my future self, the most likely reader of this missive in any case.

So I have created a repository for memory, a madeleine to jog a return to June 21, 2018. Or perhaps, as Annie Dillard says, I have begun obliterating the day from memory in order to save only the written versions of events. "After you've written, you can no longer remember anything but the writing." She seems lamentably resigned to this fact, but in my particular case, I am inclined to think there is no big loss, given the almost certain probability that this summer solstice would fade into a generalized nothing just as all the others have. So I welcome the supplanting of experience by its selective translation, these small parts of my day transformed into a more particularly durable form.

As Eduardo Galeano taught me when I first spoke with him (in downtown Montevideo at Café Brasilero one December summer solstice or thenabouts), reality consists not only of the external nontextual; our writing, too, is real: "We begin with the moment an act happens in reality, outside the author's head, and then the author reproduces in himself what happened outside himself. Then this idea, this reproduction of the act inside the author's head, also becomes part of reality. The original act, which comes directly or indirectly from reality, is transfigured in the process of creation."

Elsewhere, near and far from me, my fellow beings spun other Pokéstops and attended other wedding receptions; joyed and sorrowed at goals and misses; sat writing staring at other mountains, or oceans, or forests, or brick walls, or trash heaps; made futile efforts to stave off the encroaching entropy. Others danced and drummed and sang, some at monuments long ago constructed to mark the northernmost place where the sun stood still in the sky. Still others suffered in common and unspeakable ways. Underneath us all, the earth wobbled slightly as it spun unaccountably fast, imperceptibly fast, as it continued its seemingly interminable revolutions, barely noting the significance of once again leaning fully toward the sun.

Listening (feat. Mary Cappello)

I am none of those who write of grand issues, who peek behind the scenes of our systems to diagnose and prescribe, whose important ideas change minds and hearts and lead to action. Thus I have been struggling with what I might write here, and now, mostly because I am a frivolous forty-something writer of no real consequence, a person who recognizes that, while I quite enjoy writing, and I am deeply grateful to live now and here in a time and place that allow me to earn a living not quite as a writer but as a teacher of writing, my essays serve very little purpose and affect very few lives and only in very small and temporary ways. In the introduction to *The Best American Essays 1997*, Ian Frazier wrote that one of his favorite essays is Martin Luther King's "I Have a Dream" speech ("an essay from [King] was above all an action—from the anger and sense of injustice that impelled it, through the disciplined prose with which it meant to tear injustice down"). Mine, though it's predictably impossible to choose, might be Charles Lamb's "New Year's Eve," in which the forty-something writer foresees his own nonexistence and cowers, pining at length for the pleasures of life he will then miss: "sun, and sky, and breeze, and solitary walks, and summer holidays, and the greenness of fields, and the delicious juices of meats and fishes, and society, and the cheerful glass, and candle-light, and fire-side conversations, and innocent vanities, and jests . . ." Unlike many of his contemporaries, who celebrate the new start afforded by the new year, Lamb claims,

I am none of those who—

Welcome the coming, speed the parting guest.

I am naturally, beforehand, shy of novelties; new books, new faces, new years,—from some mental twist which makes it difficult in me to face the prospective.

Which phrase inspired this essay's opening. So that's a little essay-referential game I play with myself when I'm writing, to no benefit whatsoever other than my own amusement.

I am also a middle-aged, middle-class, religious white male, nearly all of the demographic categories that recently slaughtered my vision of progress by electing the most spectacularly dangerously unqualified person imaginable to "lead" our country. I don't know what to do. It has been my belief that even writing his name was a perilous act, because in the digital age the old adage "any publicity is good publicity" is multiplied tenfold, given the amoral algorithms crawling the ether to determine and reproduce what is popular, with no care whether it be for good or ill. So, with Lamb, and with many of my friends, I look with dread upon the coming new year. I would like to believe in "moral evolution" as my dear friend Brian Doyle believed, and yet this event has come as such a blow.

Nearly two hundred years ago, soon after Lamb wrote his new-year's reflections, William Hazlitt, upon noticing and deciding not to kill a spider, launched his most enduring (and least endearing) essay, "On the Pleasure of Hating." His thesis states that "The spirit of malevolence survives the practical exertion of it," suggesting that though we may learn to keep our gut reactions in check, we remain, at core, tribal and reactionary, responding to deep urges that betray our noble public personas. Perhaps ingeniously, but almost certainly ingenuously, Hazlitt provides a prescription: "It will ask another hundred years of fine writing and hard thinking to cure us of the prejudice and make us feel towards this ill-omened tribe with something of 'the milk of human kindness,' instead of their own shyness and venom." In the past, Hazlitt was always talking about spiders here, but when I read the essay again for the umpteenth time recently, I felt I suddenly understood that he was talking about how we treat one another. Certainly that's what the rest of the essay is about, so it makes perfect sense. But I ask myself: Did he truly believe that fine writing and hard thinking could cure us of our prejudices? Haven't I often preached that reading and writing essays can make us better people, more empathetic, more compassionate and kind? Of course, with his "hundred years" prediction, he's way off, though I wonder if he's right in spirit, or for a smaller "us" to be cured.

As this essay of mine originally occupied a spot in the Essay Daily Advent Calendar, I would be remiss not to at least try to make a metaphorical connection. I will do this not with a nod to the liturgical year, but with a sidestep to Joan Didion's borrowing/reimagining of W. B. Yeats's apocalyptic-adventish poem, "The Second Coming," which asks "what rough beast, its hour come round at last, / Slouches towards Bethlehem to be born?" As with so much prophesy, we find its fulfillment always. In 1967, Didion felt its lines "reverberat[ing] in [her] inner ear as if they were surgically implanted there." She says, "The widening gyre, the falcon which does not hear the falconer, the gaze blank and pitiless as the sun; those have been . . . the only images against which much of what I was seeing and hearing and thinking seemed to make any pattern." Read the opening of her essay, with its bankruptcies and casual killings and disappearances and children never to learn "the games that had held society together," and you might think she'd seen our day. Perhaps she had. She surely sees it now. Or perhaps she sees the inevitable entropic result of all she saw fifty years ago, an "atomization" which, she says, left her "paralyzed by the conviction that writing was an irrelevant act."

The conviction that writing was an irrelevant act. And this was Joan Didion! What hope is there for the rest of us writers?

This past summer, when the current political reality seemed only a bizarre, inappropriate joke, I spoke at length with my dear friend Mary Cappello, whose compassion and wisdom are unmatched. We were recording our conversation for later transcription and editing into a *Fourth Genre* "inter-review." I felt (we both felt) that the turns and meanders, the profundities expansions were edifying and inspiring in ways few conversations are. We looked forward to sharing the highlights. But we discovered that the electronic recording had failed, leaving a corrupt file that captured only the last half hour of what had been a two-and-a-half-hour discussion. We were disappointed, of course, deflated even, realizing that there would be no record for others and only summary-in-memory for ourselves. We spoke again a week later, via Skype, with backup recorders on both ends, and this new conversation (the edited version, also edifying, but differently so) did appear in print, but that first one resounded only in its moment and was muffled into the background almost as soon as its sound waves troubled and then stilled.

In writing this essay, hoping for some inspiration about what to do, wanting writing to be a relevant act, I recalled that one of the topics Mary and I touched on in that first conversation was the value of writing like ours: essays published in small-circulation journals and later in university-press books, literary think pieces that meander and apprehend a menagerie of ideas toward inconclusiveness. I had mentioned to Mary the lament I began this essay with, that I am a frivolous writer who admires but cannot seem to write culturally conscious and politically active essays, like Martin Luther King's, which approach social ills head on and, with power and grace, signal a way forward.

To my great joy, I found that Mary's response begins exactly where the recording became coherent for a half hour. This is what she said:

> Do our books not tackle social issues? Not head on. That doesn't mean that they don't contribute to changing the landscape from which social issues emerge. . . . If [an essay is] going to help a reader to think and respond with you in concert, you're modeling a different kind of response to being in the world. This is what writers do. That's what I want in great writing.

> If that man had a different surround sound, would he have been encouraged to buy a gun? And the people who trampled the guard at Walmart: they all must have been tuned in to the same station. All it takes is trying to listen differently, being

encouraged to listen differently. What is it we do if not ask people to try to listen differently?

Although I've known about, read from, and written for the Essay Daily site for years, just now, for the first time, I heard its name, "Essay Daily," as an imperative or at least suggestion, like the exhortation at the end of Mass: *Go forth to love and serve the Lord and each other.*

Solutions

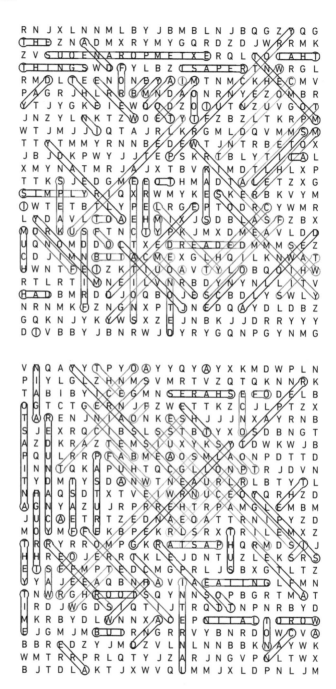

M A N O T E S H I T W P D P N G Y G T Z J T Z Q Y B
V N Y W V T N N W J N J J Q I S D I M A K P B E M R
R X T K Z D J N I W K M G L N G J T P S P Y A Y B N
Y I B X W N T I N E L O D N I T R Y E E B R W T T Z
L O N X V I M D W A S T E S G O E D N L S H L P J N
G U Z L M S G D M R Y V N M C L N T D Z E G D M G L
X S Q E D D T I M B Y N N T L R E I R R T P D J D X
L L E M L R J R Y J G L M O P R O Q F Q D L Y E Q S
N Y T E B O V Q L X N L W P T N T S N M R R C K S Q
E A A T L W B L K R T I Q A N H N G S Q B O E E D Y
T T L B G B D S T O N E I R E A D L X W R Q L T N N
T O U J Z M M M M G N N H T I W W L P A O M Z A A I
I P C D P B Q U K R M L Y T W W L Z T T R R M B N L
R D L N D M S L J E I N X X L M W E J A K W D L P R
W D A A G E P U N O X R J D L L O Z H N W T T K T N
D Q C M S M W T L D D S P E L T J N J Y O G X J M B
N L T U J M S O E T H D H M D E L R A L T H O U G H
A D A R B J W G R E I T O L P E H O B D Y Q G L N R
H C L E N Z A O N D T M Z E I Y R T N E D K Z D T T
D G L H V G M L D A S N A S D S E O Y Y H Z J F E P
N O I R N O S A L L Z E U T K M H F F N M I E W X Y
U O T E T U T C D K E R A M E Y T A I T Y L N R G V
O D S H D N O G V Y E Y Y R W L A L R N E Y P D T V
F J E O E V W A S L N B R Z C E F R T E D N Y L R R
Y R K M E T L M J P P J J A H H M M Y L D X V M R Z
B U Y Q M W Y N Q R L W L S L N B B P R K V L Z Y L

O O S B Y Y N L M L K T M B Q Z R D K C X T L X B B
H R E J M B E R T V R G W G Y M Z Z A O M L T M O W
T T U N R T D D P Q N T P R D Z R C M N A T L R V L
I H G S M V D T N D D L E L Y D O Y B T Y M G A V Q
M O A B E L I Q R N B V N Q D P Y A T A Y E L V P J
E G E M F G H M J A O N O Q H N N Z D I S R A N M G
T R L O Z D A Y J C N T P O Q T Y Z J N V R E X L T
H A I B R Y N U S Y T S N N W O N K N U I S J V H K
Y P N L Z R T I G T T I L D N M R Q Q A Q T N A E A
P H D N G A D N S N E S G A S E R U T C U R T S T J
Y I O T N R R X Y S A G I V T M S I E Y W A K V Y Z
R C L R I B I T M J L L L H N E O E L N Z Y E L R K
A A E E T I D S B J N T Y X P N D R D L I R B B L M
M L N A I L V L O M T J I R S E D T F U Y G K Y Y Z
I V C S A T D D L L P D P M N R R M H R L T A L T N
D E E U W S E N S E L E S S A R B M G O P C H M N Y
S R B R A D D W T A M T R P G G E N I O U C N Y I G
J B Y E M M W B T M O H N J K V I V J T U G B I I R
W A S S E R P X E I D A Y Y I H D N E S T R H V N T
S L N E D D A M N D S T O F T N T O E E Q E E T L I
J E O L U O W J N S I N Y Y L W E H R D H N D M Y S
Q K V A L D J W L T W T R M L L O V D M B T D P Y J
R Z L L X P O Z Z Z N E O J L L A R E Y A O R S B T
Q X M T E N G R D E V T D T J T K Z D J B N T T I W
T P L Q K S W Q W E R J L B N Y B L R S Y E T T P L
Y W J D J G Y T M G R N V M D I T K W B M B L J K W

Lightning Source UK Ltd.
Milton Keynes UK
UKHW040952100320
359953UK00012B/363